AGASTYA
IN THE
TAMIL LAND

AGASTYA
IN THE
TAMIL LAND

K. N. SIVARAJA PILLAI

GYAN

Published by

Gyan Publishing House
5, Ansari Road
Daryaganj, New Delhi-110002
Phone: 011-47034999, 9811692060
E-mail: books@gyanbooks.com

Distribution Network
gyanbooks.com
India, USA, Canada, UK, Australia, France

ISBN : 978-81-212-4491-6 (HB)
First Published, 1930

2nd Impression 2020

Printed at: Gyan Press, Delhi.

Agastya in the Tamil Land
Author: K. N. Sivaraja Pillai

CONTENTS.

AGASTYA IN THE TAMIL LAND

Introduction.

No tradition is so widespread throughout the length and breadth of the Tamil country as that concerning sage Agastya and his numerous exploits. Of all the mythic, semi-historic and historic personages of the Aryan annals, who have figured in South Indian History, Agastya has occupied the foremost place and secured the largest homage of the cultured and the masses alike. He meets us from the very start of Aryan History, being a composer of certain hymns of the earliest of the Vēdas, the Ṛg Vēda. Still he seems to have been not included amongst the seven holy sages, the *Prajāpatis*, or the progenitors of the human race. These were Gōtama, Bharadwāja, Viśwāmitra, Jamadagni, Vasiṣṭha, Kāśyapa and Atri. Even later Purāṇas, like the *Vāyu* and the *Viṣṇu*, which have amplified the list of the primitive sages by including Bhṛgu and Dakṣa, have only quietly passed Agastya over. This circumstance may lend some colour of support to the doubt whether Agastya is not after all the sage of a later day. However that be, posterity has made ample amends for this omission by raising him to a still higher position and assigning him a place among the Stars. The Star Canopus, which sheds its brilliance in the Southern heavens, is believed to be none other than the austere Sage Agastya, the semi-divine benefactor of the human race, who has been thus honoured by a grateful posterity.

His birth.

It is no wonder that this famous figure should have become the centre of multifarious mythic accretions. His advent into this world, equally with his translation to the starry heavens, falls beyond human belief and even conception. He is known as *Kalaśaja, Kalaśīsuta, Kumbhayōni, Kumbhasambhava, Ghaṭōdbhava* (the pot-born), from the fact that he was born from the seed of Mitra received and preserved in a pot. The story runs that once upon a time both Mitra and Varuṇa had a sort of love contest in respect of the heavenly damsel Ūrvaśī and that they could not do anything more than depositing their fertile seed, one in a pot and the other in the sea. In time, Agastya was born from the pot and Vasiṣṭha, one of the reputed Saptarṣis, started his life from the sea. From this divine parentage Agastya is called also Maitra-Vāruṇi and Ourvaśīya. There are variations of this story in later traditions; but it serves no purpose to recount them here. One fact is plain enough from Agastya's biography, that to ordinary mortals his birth is as mysterious as his translation to a star. From the trend of the primitive Aryan mind to revel in the supernatural, one should be inclined to be cautious, to the extent of even scepticism, in seeking to reach a nucleus of truth in an overgrowth of materials legendary to the core. Still one may be allowed the consolation that even after discounting the value of the miraculous and mythical chaff in the life of this sage, there may yet remain certain solid grains of human history which could be garnered into the historic store of the ancient Aryans. How far and in what manner that can be effected without doing violence to the demands of normal human reason remains a problem to this day.

Earlier Myths.

The myths that have gathered round this Aryan sage fall into two broad classes, the earlier and the later. His so-called Exodus to the South from Āryāvarta serves to divide the incidents into the Aryan and the Dravidian group of myths. From the point of view of the historical investigator, there is hardly any ground for distinctive choice between them. Both run on parallel lines and are steeped in the miraculous through and through. The Himalaya mountain of the northern myth is replaced by the Pothiyil of the South; Agastya's composition of many Ṛg Vedic hymns and medical works in Samscrit is answered by his numerous mystic and medical treatises in Tamil; his effort in bringing down the Ganges with the consent of Śiva (*vide* Kāśi Kāṇḍam) finds an echo in his getting Tāmraparṇi from Śiva and his bargaining with God Gaṇēśa for Kāvēri; his seat in Benares seems to be replaced by his abode in Badāmi, known as Dakṣiṇa Kāśi; his marriage with Lopāmudrā, the daughter of a Vidarbha King, has also a parallel in his wedding of Kāvēri, the daughter of King Kavēra; and taking into consideration the curses, which had issued from his spiritual armoury in the north, his curse of Tolkāppiyar, his own student, shows unmistakably how the dwarf sage—for on account of his diminutive size he was known as *Kuṟumuṉi* also—kept true to his old habits, in the far-away South. This parallelism is sufficient to establish that the southern myths are largely mere echoes of the northern and may be presumed to have been due either to a pure Aryan source in the South or to a Dravidian origin borrowing its *motif* and whole inspiration from the Aryan. Incidentally, it may be interesting to refer to some recent attempts to make out of this far-famed Aryan protagonist an indigenous saint of blue Dravidian blood. The fanciful theorizers, who have been led to do this, have been driven, in the absence of sober grounds, to invoke to their aid Philology—a frail reed to lean upon. They connect Agastya, or Akattiyaṉ in Tamil, with *Akatti* (அகத்தி) tree and elaborate for the occasion a fable that the Saint being a physician himself was very fond of *Akatti* and had it planted round his hermitage. Here we find myth opposing myth and the ends of natural justice more than satisfied. But, apart from any dialectical victory, the question for us to consider is whether Agastya could be made to claim a Dravidian parentage. If Agastya were a Dravidian by birth, one might justifiably ask what necessity there was in the Southerner to duplicate the incidents which had befallen the life of his northern compeer. Mere accident can scarcely be supposed to explain away so many points of contact as we find in the life-history of this interesting couple.

Reflections.

Taking the myths as a whole, a few points strike us as worthy of mention here. Naturally enough the name of this antique figure has been intertwined to a large extent with nature-myths of the remotest antiquity. His coming down to the South to equalise the Southern Hemisphere with the Northern in the tilted scale of the heavenly balance, his suppression of the Vindhya mountains and his drinking up the ocean dry may be connected with certain astronomical and geological phenomena (of which we have no knowledge at present), coming as cataclysms once in a way to disturb the otherwise uniform flow of natural events. Setting these aside, we find that by far the greater number of the miraculous incidents which fill his life fall under the class of curses of unerring potency. Indeed so free was he with his curses and so deep-rooted was the instinct of cursing in him that one might be tempted to dub him the Cursing Saint *par excellence.* He was born a dwarf and what he lacked in stature he seems to have more than made up by his acquisition of extraordinary powers bordering on the miraculous. His temper was at no time balanced and under the slightest provocation would rush into an irate mood of destructive proclivity. Indra, Nahuṣa, Ūrvaśī, Ghṛtācī, Madiyanandai, Tāṭakā, Sunda, Krauñca, Maṇimanda, Lōpāmudrā, and Tholkāppiyar had all to pay heavy penalties, one way or another, for provoking him. A beneficent mood too he seems to have had; but very rarely could the saint be prevailed upon to dole out his benedictions to this sinful world. It may be charitable to suppose that a reforming saint, as our sage was reputed to have been, must have been under special necessities at that remote period to whip a wicked world into some sort of acceptable moral order. A good deal, however, could be forgiven in one who had become the centre of light and leading by sitting at the feet of God himself—Śiva, Muruga, the Sun-God, all had a hand in his instruction and training—and imbibing knowledge for the guidance of erring humanity. His very mediation between God and Man may be urged as a ground for measuring him by a standard other than what we adopt in the judgment of ordinary mortals. Let alone his activities in Northern India, the events which mark his progress towards the South have an interest all their own for the student of South Indian History. Hence these deserve to be studied in greater detail.

His Exodus to the South.

Geographically his exodus to the Peninsular India divides itself into three distinct strata. The earliest finds him lodged in the Agastyāśrama, a few miles north of Nāsik, the ancient Pañcavaṭī, on the northern borders of the Daṇḍakāraṇya Forest. His marriage of Lopāmudrā, the daughter of the Vidarbha King and Rama's first interview with him take place here. The second stratum begins with his residence at Malakūṭa, three miles east of Badāmi (the ancient Vātāpipura) otherwise known as Dakṣiṇakāśī, in the Kaladgi District of the Bombay

Presidency. We must remember that this new residence is about three hundred miles down south from his Nāsik Āśrama of the first period. Agastya's eating up Vātāpi and his destruction of Ilvala (known also as Vilvala) may be referred to this period of his sojourn in the South. The third stratum of stories gathers round him at Pothiyil, known also as Malaya, one of the southernmost promontories of the Western Ghats, in the Pāṇḍya country. With such a residence in the very centre of the foremost Tamil Nāṭu of those days, he is credited with having founded the first Tamil Academy and having presided over it, besides writing an Extensive Tamil Grammar and sundry other works on medicine, mysticism, and even magic. Tradition, however, does not leave him here in his southernmost home, about eight hundred miles away from his Nāsik Āśrama. Two more strata of legends are added by making him cross the seas. In the fourth epoch, we find him landed in the Indonesian Islands in the East, where he is said to have visited Barhiṇadvīpa (Borneo), Kuśa Dvīpa, and Varāha Dvīpa. Here too he appears to have taken up his abode in the Mahā Malaya Hill in Malaya Dvīpa. The fifth and last stage is reached when he is made to cross over to the mainland and enter Siam and Cambodia. It was here, at the end of his ever-lengthening journey eastwards, he had to marry a local beauty, Yaśomati by name, and leave by her a royal progeny among whom King Yaśovarmā was an outstanding personage. Leaving out of account the exploits of his trans-Indian tour, which happily many of his Indian followers in the mainland are unaware of to this day, the other layers of tradition, which cling to his achievements on the Indian soil, have all been laid one over another in the course of a few centuries and have thus grown into a vast pile by themselves. To make this 'confusion worse confounded', the later Paurānic writers also have spun all sorts of amazing tales of mystery and imagination round this Aryan sage without an eye to smooth away inconsistencies and escape contradictions. Probably they may have thought that the sage was too great a man to sink under the weight of their legendary lore.

As a first step in the so-called Aryanisation[1] of Dakṣiṇāpatha (Southern India) and Further India, the northern tradition which has gathered round his hermitage near Daṇḍakāraṇya gives us a valuable clue.

---

1. If by 'civilization' one means the possession of a body of literature, religion and philosophy, as is too often done by certain Sanskritists, then Dravidian India could be truly spoken of as aryanised. If, on the other hand, the term signified, as it should, very much more than these very late accomplishments, as for instance man's control of Nature by wresting from it not only the necessities but the comforts and conveniences of life by a well-developed and well-ordered system of arts in almost every department of human pursuit, and the consequent amelioration of man's estate both in his individual and corporate existence in society by all the devices at his command and by all the efforts he is capable of, then more than three-fourths of the belongings of the present-day life must go to the credit of an indigenous civilization the Dravidian has inherited from his ancestors. Take for instance, two of the prime arts of life, Agriculture and Architecture. Where is the Aryanisation in them ? To speak still of the Aryanisation of Dravidian India, in the extremely limited sense, is to lose the right historical perspective and growing even unfair to the substantial contributions of the Dravidians to the stock of the present-day South Indian civilization. Even in the field of letters, religion and philosophy, no student of history will be inclined to discount the characteristic share of the Dravidians, although it may not compare in quantity favourably with that of the Aryan nation.

As at present, even at that early time, secular movements, of which colonisation of countries may be taken as a type, went in the wake of missionary enterprise and Agastya's trying to plant the Aryan religious rites, amongst the alien tribes of the South, only furnished the opportunity for the later expansion of the Aryans into the Southern region. It would not be true to say that Agastya himself was conscious, at the time, of the far-reaching consequences of his acts pursued for other purposes than land occupation. Nevertheless, being the first man who had pioneered the race into a new country of unmeasured potentiality, he should naturally come to be looked upon as a benefactor of his race, deserving their highest homage and worship. There is absolutely little or no difficulty from the Aryan point of view in explaining away the high veneration in which Agastya's name is still held. But the real problem begins only when we try to approach the subject from the Dravidian side. It is inconceivable how a whole race could be brought round to extol a foreign leader of men as the type of perfection in learning, wisdom, and saintliness and accept him as their own spiritual overlord and guide. Here, at any rate, we find the extraordinary phenomenon of almost the entire Tamil race of the present day enthroning Agastya, an Aryan Ṛṣi, in a rank little removed from that of divinity and paying him homage as to one of their own kith and kin. Is it possible, one may ask, for a race to exhibit such utter lack of race-consciousness as is here displayed? It may be doubted whether the attempt to make a Dravidian out of the Aryan sage has not been done with a view to cut the Gordian knot, here presented. Howevermuch race-consciousness may feel flattered by this daring feat, it is a foregone conclusion that no scholar of any standing will be found to stake his reputation on the acceptance of this new-fangled theory.

After all, the problem is not so hopeless as it appears at first sight. In fact, it serves the great purpose of driving us to revalue the data on which the Agastya legend has been built up in the Tamil land.

Appraisement of Tradition.

In all societies, Tradition stands as the natural background of history. Authentic history can scarcely be said to arise before the invention of writing and the vast period in which man had been evolving from a primitive state of existence is one of haze, if not darkness, from the standpoint of recorded history. The indefatigable labours of Anthropologists and Archaeologists have doubtless resulted in marshalling other records than those in writing, which throw fairly good light on the life of man in prehistoric times; but these unfortunately do not cover the whole extent of man's spiritual evolution. Except the fitful glimpses afforded by the artifacts left behind by the primitive man into some aspects of his inner life, we have scarcely anything to enable us to read the whole extent and colour of it. Many chapters in the spiritual evolution of man must thus remain sealed for ever. Scientific approach becoming impracticable here, at least Tradition may be expected to step in to throw a few rays into the dark corridors of by-gone times. And as a matter of fact, the primitive history of every race and tribe is found to consist entirely of Traditions whose value may vary according to circumstances. The scientific historian is bound not to throw them overboard *en masse* but to sift them carefully and scrupulously, to arrive at whatever modicum of truth they may contain. The task of separating the ore from the dross is, however, a difficult one and few indeed can hope to succeed in it who does not bring with him an irreproachable scientific temper and method and a sympathetic imagination withal. In valuing traditions generally, one has to see first, whether they satisfy the most important pre-requisite, absence of internal inconsistencies and contradictions and secondly, whether they can claim an unbroken continuity with the remote past. Let us see how the Agastya tradition fares judged as it should be by these fundamental tests.

Antiquity of Tradition.

However ancient this tradition has been made to look like in later times, certainly it cannot be anterior to the founding of the earliest settlement of the Aryans beyond the Vindhya mountains, which for a long time stood as an impenetrable barrier in their way to the South. The north-eastern and south-western ends of this chain of mountains were known to the inhabitants of Āryāvarta as Pāriyātra, because they marked the boundary of their *yātrā* or range of communication. The tide of Aryan Migration which was thus stemmed in, towards the south, flowed on in an easterly direction along the course of the Ganges up to its very mouth in the Bay of Bengal. Later on, it seems to have overflowed in this corner taking a south-westerly course as far as Utkala—the modern Orissa. Reference is made in Aitarēya Brāhmaṇa to the Sage Viśwāmitra having condemned by a curse the progeny of fifty of his sons to live on the borders of the Aryan settlement and these were "the Āndhras, Puṇḍras, Śabaras, Pulindas, and Mutibās and the descendants of Viśwāmitra formed a large proportion of the Dasyus."[1]

---

1. Aitarēya Brāhmaṇa, VII, 18.

cf. Prof. Max Muller's conclusion in pp. 334—335 of his *History of Ancient Sanskrit Literature.*

" At all events the Taittirīya Āryaṇyaka represents the latest period in the development of the Vedic religion, and shows a strong admixture of post-vedic ideas and names. The same applies also to several parts of the Taittirīya Brāhmaṇa, the last part of which does not belong to Taittiri, but is

These tribes are referred to in the later epics and the Purāṇās as occupying the country to the South of the Vindhyas, beginning from a little to the north of the mouth of the Godāvarī in the east to the mouth of the Narmadā in the west. But this knowledge of a few tribes to the South-east of the Vindhya range on the part of the author of the Aitarēya Brāhmaṇa hymn does not count for much. For, Pāṇini, whose date on the most liberal calculation[1] of Dr. R. G. Bhandarkar is taken to be 700 B. C., makes mention in his sūtras of Kacca, Avanti, Kōsala, Karūṣa, and Kaliṅga as the farthest countries in the South. Dr. Bhandarkar writes "Supposing that the non-occurrence of the name of any country farther south in Pāṇini's work is due to his not having known it, a circumstance, which looking to the many names of places in the North that he gives appears probable, the conclusion follows that in his time the Aryans were confined to the north of the Vindhya but

---

ascribed to Kaṭha, the same Muni to whom the beginning of the Āryaṇyaka is said to have been revealed. There are some traces which would lead to the supposition that the Taittirīya Veda had been studied particularly in the South of India, and even among people which are still considered as un-Aryan in the Brāhmaṇa of the Ṛg Vēda. In the Taittirīya Āraṇyaka different readings are mentioned which are no longer ascribed to different Śākhās but to certain countries in the South of India, like those of the Drāvidas, Āndhras and Karnāṭakas. This fact by itself would throw some doubt on the antiquity and genuineness of the class of Vedic writings at least in that form in which we now possess them."

1. For instance, Dr. Washburn Hopkins of the Yale University tries to ascribe Pāṇini to the 3rd century B. C. He writes : " But no evidence has yet been brought forward to show conclusively that Pāṇini lived before the 3rd century B.C." Vide *The Great Epic of India*, p. 391.

did not proceed or communicate with the northern-most portion of the Eastern Coast, not by crossing that range, but by avoiding it by taking an easterly course."[1] Thus then Agastya piercing the Vindhya in his colonising expedition to the South cannot be dated earlier than 700 B. C. Taking next the references made to Vidarbha, the Berars, in both the Epics, the Rāmāyaṇa and the Mahābhārata, Dr. Bhandarkar gives out as his considered opinion that this State was the oldest Aryan province in the southern country.[2] He does not tell us whether it was founded by the Aryans who came from the East or by the followers of Agastya who cut across the Vindhyas from the North. It may, however, be presumed from the tradition that Agastya gave the girl Lōpāmudrā to a king of Vidarbha to be brought up by him and afterwards claimed her for his wife, that that kingdom must have existed sometime before Agastya's entering into a marital alliance with one of its Kings. Even supposing that the two epics began their existence at about 500 B.C.—and there are scholars who bring down the dates of the composition of these Epics much lower—the Kingdom of Vidarbha must have started into existence sometime between 700 and 500 B. C. And in this interval also Agastya's meeting of the Vidarbha King must be placed. We shall not be far wrong then if we date the beginning of Agastya's colonising career somewhere about 600 B. C. If, on the other hand, we give weight to the arguments of scholars that till 100 B. C. these celebrated epics have been undergoing material additions in successive recensions—and in fact the force of these arguments cannot be lightly set aside—we may have to revise the date to a still lower level.

---

1. Dr. Bhandarkar's *Early History of Deccan*, pp. 12-13.
2. Dr. Bhandarkar's *Early History of Deccan*, p. 7.

Thus 600 B. C. is a fairly early enough date. It was about this period that the hero of the Ramāyaṇa met Agastya, in his Āśram near Nāsik, the ancient Pañcavaṭī. The country to the south of Vidarbha, the site of the modern Mahārāṣṭra, was then an impenetrable forest known as Daṇḍākāraṇyam infested by fierce animals and wild tribes.[1] If, however, a higher antiquity is claimed for the epics, we have to simply leave them aside as incapable of being brought into relationship with the historical incidents of Aryan immigration into South India. However unserviceable these epics may be for chronological purposes of a positive historic character, an unexpected light is thrown upon this tract of time by the early Greek writers. I shall refer only to two of the earliest of them, Ktesias of Knidos and Megasthenes, both of the 4th century B. C. The India of these writers was only India north of the Vindhyas. Had they received any information about the southern peninsula, certainly they would have included it in their otherwise elaborate accounts. Not only this, the impression they seem to have formed is that from Pātāḷē at the mouth of the Indus in the West to Gangē at the mouth of the Ganges in the East there ran an almost straight coast-line washed by the Southern Ocean. This ignorance on the part of the early writers, including Ktesias, may have been due to various reasons and need not concern us here ; but when we find it pervading the writing of so careful a writer as Megasthenes, who lived at the court of Pāṭaliputra and had at his command all the sources of informa-

1. Compare with this the observations of such late writers as the author of the 'Periplus of the Erythrean Sea' and the Chinese Travellers of the 5th and the 7th Centuries after Christ. They refer to the extreme difficulty of getting by land into S. India.

tion available at the time, his omission of South India becomes truly significant. It could be ascribed to no other reason than the patent one, that peninsular India was then an unknown region in the North and hence the sources Megasthenes must have tapped for his account could not have furnished him with any information regarding the South. Even Kātyāyana's reference to Pāṇḍya, and Cōḻa in his Vārtika marks only the first faint glimmerings of an imperfect acquaintance with South India about 350 B. C. which broadens subsequently into clear knowledge sometime about 150 B. C., the time of Patañjali. Thus then the testimony of Sanskrit Literature and the early Greek writers places beyond a doubt that Southern India about 400 B. C. was almost a *terra incognita* to the Northern Aryans[1]. Viewed in this

---

1. This conclusion is more than clinched by the finding of Prof. A. A. Macdonell in his *History of Sanskrit Literature:* pp. 8 9.

"The History of Ancient Indian Literature naturally falls into two main periods. The first is the Vedic, which beginning perhaps as early as 1,500 B. C. extends in its latest phase to about 200 B. C. In the former half of the Vedic Age the character of its literature was creative and poetical while the centre of culture lay in the territory of the Indus and its tributaries, the modern Punjab ; in the latter half, Literature was theologically speculative in matter and prosaic in form, while the centre of intellectual life had shifted to the valley of the Ganges. Thus in the course of the Vedic Age Aryan civilization had overspread the whole of Hindustan proper, the vast tract extending from the mouths of the Indus to those of the Ganges, bounded on the North by the Himalayas, and on the South by the Vindhya range. The second period concurrent with the final off-shoots of Vedic Literature and closing with the Mahammadan conquest after 1,000 A. D. is the Sanskrit period strictly speaking. In a certain sense, owing to the continued literary use of Sanskrit mainly for the composition

light the very detailed and elaborate references to the South that we find in the two epics should be taken as nothing better than subsequent interpolations.

Agastya in the Tamil Country.

Next, let us see whether there is anything in the later Greek writers or Tamil Classical Literature, coming about the first two centuries after Christ. There is absolutely nothing about this sage in any of the writings we have now taken up for consideration. Ptolemy makes mention of Bettigo,[1] the Pothigai, a variant of Pothiyil, but passes on without any allusion to the resident sage. His silence is striking and suggestive if considered with the silence of the Tamil Classical Literature taken as a whole.

Except *Paripāḍal*[2], which belongs very likely to the sixth or the seventh century A. D., not a single work is there among the Śaṅgam works—works shorn of course of the legendary embellishments of later commentators—which makes any mention direct or indirect or gives us any clue by name or implication to the life of this sage, his works or even his very existence. In *Pattuppāṭṭu*

---

of commentaries, this period may be regarded as coming down to the present day. During this second epoch Brahman culture was introduced and overspread the Southern portion of the continent called the Dekkhan or the " South."

1. *Vide* Appendix I.

2. Judged by the style and sentiments of the poems contained in this work, few critics, I believe, will contend for its high antiquity. The opinion is common amongst Tamil scholars that this late production was included in the Sangam collection of writings to do duty for the missing genuine Paripāḍals of old. Mr. R. S. Narayanaswami Aiyar, B. A., B. L., from certain astronomical calculations, suggests 372 A. D., as the probable date of the composition of this Poem. *Vide* Chentamil, Vol. 19, p. 384.

(The Ten Idylls) no poet has referred to Agastya or his civilising activity in behalf of the Tamil race. Nor is there any reference to Pothiyil as the seat of Agastya in the very heart of the Tamil country. No doubt the word (பொதியில்) Pothiyil occurs in *Tirumurugāṟṟuppaṭai, Maturaikkāñci,* etc., but in all of them it means a common place of meeting. Likewise, excepting *Paripāṭal* as already stated, in none of the works composing Eṭṭutokai (The Eight Collections) is there any reference to Agastya. In places where the Pothiyil hill is mentioned in *Puṟanāṉūṟu* (*vide* stanzas 2 and 128) or in *Naṟṟiṇai* (*vide* stanza 379) Agastya's name does not appear. In certain texts a connection between the hill and the Pāṇḍya King and not the sage is all that is brought about. It is worthy of note in this connection how Nacchiṉārkkiṉiyar, a late commentator, tries to popularise the Agastya cult by twisting a few lines of verse in *Maduraikkāñci* from their most obvious and natural meaning, and thereby almost manufacturing a reference to the sage Agastya. Here are the lines :—

"தென்னவற் பெயரிய துன்னருந் துப்பிற்
றொன்முது கடவுட் பின்னர் மேய
வரைத்தாழருவிப் பொருப்பிற் பொருந." —மதுரைக்காஞ்சி.

Its translation is as follows :—Oh! War-like Prince, lord of the hill resounding with waterfalls, and known as the 'Southern King' (by pre-eminence) and, in point of unapproachable prowess, standing second only to that ancient primal Being (Śiva) himself. The adjectival phrase தென்னவற் பெயரிய may also be taken as qualifying தொன்முதுகடவுள் and interpreted as the god who subdued by his might Yama, the Lord of the South. The term Mutukaṭavuḷ முதுகடவுள் is herein used to distinguish Śiva from Muruga or Kumāra, the youthful deity, his son. Nacchiṉārkkiṉiyar makes 'Mutukaṭavuḷ' denote Agastya and 'Theṉṉavaṉ,' Rāvaṇā, and imports into the lines the legend of Agastya overcoming Rāvaṇā in a musical duel and bundling him bag and baggage out of the Tamil country. The intrinsic improbabilities of this tradition apart, Nachchiṉārkkiṉiyar's interpretation of the text is altogether far-fetched and fanciful. Two familiar words have been made to shed their ordinary significations and stand for Rāvaṇā and Agastya to suit a pre-conceived theory of the commentator. Some may praise this ingenuity on the part of the commentator, but I am sure no scholar, who goes direct to the original verse, will fail to catch its natural import. The solitary reference in the line 'பொதியின் முனிவன் புரைவரை கீறி', which occurs in the 11th *Paripāṭal* and refers to the Star Canopus, receives its adequate explanation by the comparative lateness of the period of composition of that work. Barring this one intrusive instance, for which the lack of a chronological sense on the part of the redactor of the Sangam works was responsible, the whole extent of Tamil Classical Literature has not a word to say about Agastya, or his literary labours. If it is urged that a negative testimony of this sort, an *argumentum ex silentio*, is scarcely conclusive, there is the reply that the absence of reference to Agastya is certainly more than negative in the special circumstances of this case. If a reference to the Sage were to be expected anywhere at all, undoubtedly it must be in connection with the description of the Pothiyil, his mountain residence. Popular belief to this day runs on the line that the immortal Rishi is even now living in the southernmost peak of the Western Ghats. Such being the case, a poet who thinks of describing this particular hill or range should naturally be expected to allude to its saintly occupant on some occasion or another. This absence of reference to the Sage has occurred in the stanzas not of one poet only but of a number of them. Their silence seems almost conspired and is accordingly arresting. One and all of them compose their verses in utter unconsciousness of the existence of the Saint or his exploits. The only possible explanation for this phenomenon of general silence is that at that time there did not exist even a scrap of the Agastya tradition. It was all a manufacture of later days and any attempt to look for it in the pages of these early records must turn out fruitless. Thus, about the early centuries after Christ, the seed of the Agastya tradition had not yet been sown in the Tamil land. From the following three lines of a stanza of Poet Ēṇissēri Muḍamōsiyār (*Puṛanāṉūṛu*, 128), one can only conclude that the Pothiyil had not then secured the austere associations due to Agastya's saintly presence.

கழறொடி யாஅய் மழைதவழ் பொதியி
லாடுமகள் குறுகி னல்லது
பீடுகெழு மன்னர் குறுகலோ வரிதே".

Naturally the question will arise that myths being the coinage of the earliest times why the Tamil country alone should show a reverse process. Any satisfactory answer to this legitimate query forces on us the necessity of glancing a little at the racial characteristics of the Dravidians and the Aryans taken as a whole. I trust I shall not be wrong in calling the Aryans predominantly a nation of thinkers and the Dravidians characteristically a nation of doers. Not that the Aryans had not great men of action amongst them nor the Dravidians great men of thought in their ranks. But the *forte* of the national character of the two races, taken in the lump, lay one in thought and the other in action. Although the speculative and practical tendencies of a man lie mixed up beyond the possibility of a definite

Agastya tradition —its post-classical[1] origin.

1. The term classical period used in this paper refers to the period to which the extant 'Sangam works' are ascribed, *i.e.*, the few early centuries of the Christian Era.

separation, yet from almost all the biographies of individual men we learn that for one individual who shows a balanced mental make-up there are hundred others in whom either the speculative or the practical tendencies assert themselves in a more or less decisive way. This individual characteristic runs through the race also. The ancient history of the Dravidians gleaned from their earliest records and their later lives and achievements lead us to infer that they were from the beginning a highly practical race which had given itself over to sustained action in many fields of practical pursuit. They seem to have had no special aptitude for pure theorizing in any direction. They were never dreamers and builders of castles in the air. They were earnestly and intensely practical and the pragmatic success, which had crowned their activities in Agriculture, Commerce, War and Politics, could hardly have favoured anything savouring of theoretic doubt and speculation. The fabric of civilisation[1] that they thus built up is indeed a massive one, though it may not show to any great extent the glitter of certain cultural accomplishments. The Aryans who came amidst them from the North were however cast in a different mould. Their restlessness from the dawn of their history leaned towards speculation. It would be a mistake to suppose that the tendency to speculate and theorize developed in them *per saltum* at the time of the Upanishads. The Rig Vēdic hymns, though addressed to numerous deities or forces of Nature for meeting the every day wants and necessities of the race, for in short helping it in the various practical concerns in this world, bear marks, it must be admitted, of a peculiar theoretic strain in their composers. Its assiduous care in getting by rote those hymns and handing them down to the remotest posterity and its unfailing

1. *Vide* Appendix II.

performance of the rites and rituals laid down in the sacred books are certainly not the ways which will appeal to the hard matter-of-fact man wedded to the practical concerns of life. If such a people could be called practical, they were practical in a manner entirely novel, not to say unique, in the history of nations.[1] Such a race addicted to pure thought and theorizing, in their southern wandering, had to meet with a race entirely alien in modes of thought and life. Here it had to bend an intensely practical race to its own standard of perfect civilization or adapt itself to the new type. And how could even this adaptation be effected? Not certainly by meeting the Dravidians in their own ground and achieving greater success therein—an alternative they could scarcely even think of, in the case of so well-equipped a nation as the Tamils who could give them points in all Arts of peace and war. There was another and a surer way of approach. With all his achievements the Dravidian was not strong in speculation. That was the Achilles' heel, which was readily caught hold of by the incoming Aryans and their grip of it was indeed tight. Whatever be the achievements of the practical man in any field of activity, he has to bow down his head before knowledge and theory or what passed for such, which came in handy to rationalize and even illuminate practice.

---

[1] This is what Ihering says about the Aryans in his profoundly interesting work "*The Evolution of the Aryans*," p. 62.

"This also denotes the character of the people. It was a people without the least practical aptitude—the diametrical opposite of the Romans. Highly gifted intellectually they turned their tastes and thoughts to the inner-world—to speech, religion, poetry and in later times also with great results to philosophy—without feeling the necessity of applying their knowledge to the amelioration of their external conditions."

The adage 'the world is ruled by thought' appears to have been more than verified in the matter of the Dravidian-Aryan contact and the present-day mixed civilization of Southern India is the result of a healthy blend of the two fundamental elements of human nature, brought into the common stock by two different races.

It will now be clear why the earliest history of the Dravidians should bear very little trace of any mytho-poetic tendencies which lie at the bottom of all myths in general. Pre-Aryan Southern India was comparatively free from myths and with the advent of the Aryans in the South—Hindus, Buddhists and Jains,—a vast mass of mythic lore began to make its way into the land. Starting from the sectarian controversies and schisms of the various religious factions in South India, the Hindu, the Jain and the Buddhist, the Saivite, the Vaishnavite, and the Lingayet, and the many sub-divisions of these, the mythic rill seems, in a few centuries, to have swollen into a formidable torrent and literally submerged the land in the Purāṇic period which comes very close to our own times.

Agastya tradition —its post-Jainistic origin.

It was the late Mr. Venkayya, I think, who drew the attention of scholars to the existence of a Buddhist tradition that Avalōkitēsvara, a Buddhist Sage was residing in "Podalaga" or Pothiyil mountain. In fact, that tradition goes much farther than this and holds that Agastya owed to Avalōkitēśvara his initiation into knowledge as will be seen from the following stanza, appearing in the *Pāyiram* (Introduction) of *Vīrasōḻiyam*, a Tamil grammatical work.

" ஆயுங் குணத்தவ லோகிதன் பக்க லகத்தியன்கேட்
டேயும் புவனிக் கியம்பிய தண்டமி ழீங்குரைக்க
நீயு முளையோ வெனிற்கரு டன்சென்ற நீள்விசும்பி
லீயும் பறக்கு மிதற்கென் கொலோசொல்லு மேந்திழையே."

In settling the rival claims of Agastya and Avalōkitēsvara for priority in the occupation of the Pothiyil mountain and composing the first grammar of the Tamil Language, we are thrown into the very thick of the religious warfare which raged in the Tamil land just after a few centuries from the dawn of the Christian Era. From a reading of the Tamil Literature of the earliest period, it is not possible to say that one sect even before another had set foot in Tamiḻagam. Quite probably the Buddhists and the Jains may have preceded the Hindu Aryans in their arrival in the Tamil land in the first two centuries preceding the Christian Era[1]. The picture afforded by the early Tamil Literature, however, is that of a few Brahmans, orthodox and heretic, leading isolated lives and first feeling their way amongst an alien population. In stanza 166 of *Puṟaṉāṉūṟu* the Poet Avūr Mūlamkiḻār praises one Pūñchāṟṟūr Pārppāṉ Kauṇiyaṉ Viṇṇantāyaṉ for performing the twenty-one yāgās, not being misled therein by the false preachings of the heretical sectaries. Evidently the poet seems to have had the Buddhist and the Jaina Sramans in his mind as the commentator himself makes it plain. Here are the lines :—

1. This supposition receives some support from the Jain traditions and the Sravaṇa Belgōla Inscriptions, published as Volume II of the *Epigraphia Carnatika* of the Mysore State. If by 69 A. D. Buddhism can travel to China, Peninsular India down to the South may in all likelihood have been reached by that time by the zealous missionaries of these reforming sects. Jaina traditions as testified to by the Mysore Inscriptions make it clear that on account of a Twelve Years' famine in North India, Srutakēvali Bhadrabāhu, an eminent Jain monk, and his disciple, the monarch Chandragupta, led a large company of Jaina monks to the South. From Sravaṇa Belgōla they seem to have sent a party under one Visākāchārya to the Chōḷa and the Pāṇḍya countries.

" மூவேழ் துறையு முட்டின்று போகிய
இகல்கண் டோர் மிகல்சாய்மார்
மெய்யன்ன பொய்யுணர்ந்து
பொய்யோராது மெய்கொளீஇ
உரைசால் சிறப்பி னரவோர் மருக."

If this is so, the attempt to ante-date the incoming of the Hindu Aryan to the exclusion of the heretic can hardly find any support from the earliest stratum of Tamil Literature known to us. We have to infer from the circumstances of that early time that the Aryans first came into the land neither as colonists nor as guests but as missionaries to propagate their different religions and religious practices. Since the Brahmans, unlike their opponents the Buddhists and the Jains, were not at all propagandistic, one may reasonably hold that the heretics had preceded them in the South to spread the light of the new faith in countries far beyond the confines of the Aryan settlements. Whoever be the first batch of the Aryan immigrants who came to the South, they appear to have been quickly followed by others of a different religious persuasion. But they were very few in number[1] and hence could not have engaged themselves in any religious contest on a large scale. Nor were the social and political conditions of the Tamil country at that time favourable for carrying on any sort of religious propagandism. The Tamil Mūvēndar or Triumvirs (the Chēra, the Chōḷa and the Pāṇḍya Kings), from about a century perhaps earlier than the Christian era, entered on a policy of aggrandisement and were engaged in wiping out the

1. " The Brahmans of the South India appear in those days to have consisted of a number of isolated communities that were settled in separate parts of the country and that were independent each of the other."—Ptolemy's *Geography of India and Southern Asia* (Mccrindle's Translation, p. 5.)

communal chieftaincies then existing and adding their territories to their own dominions Tamiḻagam then was actually studded with a large number of village communities under their respective elders, headmen or chiefs called Kiḻārs and of tribes or congeries of such communities ruled over by their kings known as Vēḷirs or Kōs. These petty chieftaincies and kingships were, in the course of three or four centuries, swept out of existence and this involved incessant fighting and interminable forays among the many Tamil rulers concerned Such a period could scarcely have been propitious for any religious work among the people

More favourable conditions, however, ensued later on by the consolidation of the Tamil monarchies and by the stability of the social conditions it gave rise to The schismatic warfare of the North was then waged with redoubled fury in the distant South and thence it spread also to the Indonesian Islands in the Eastern Ocean It is but natural that in this fight, both parties, the orthodox and the heretical, must have resorted to every weapon in their respective armouries for gaining a victory over their opponents Apart from the bid for political power, which both had been trying to make from the beginning, the scholars too of the warring sects appear to have fed the mind of the people with all sorts of myths and miracles, as another powerful means to secure the support of the masses Of the many expedients resorted to conciliate the Tamil population and to win them over to the Hindu fold, the Agastya tradition was one and it served its purpose admirably indeed The Tamil people were treated to stories of social, religious and spiritual kinship with the more advanced Hindu Aryans of the North and were thus brought over to view the Jaina and the Buddhistic sectaries as absolutely beyond the pale of Hindu orthodoxy. The Tamil kings too were raised under priestly auspices to a position almost near godhood[1] and were given the unique privilege of tracing their descent from the Sun and Moon and counting themselves as connected with the Solar and Lunar lines of kings of the Purāṇas and the Itihāsās—people with whom they had no kinship whatsoever. Their names[2] and titles, by and by, assumed a portentous length by the adoption of sonorous Sanskrit appellations in which the hand of the family priest could be traced to have been at work. The vanity and self-importance of the rulers concerned must indeed have been considerably tickled! Methods like these employed to

---

1. "திருவுடைமன்னரைக் காணில் திருமாலைக் கண்டேனே யென்னும்" —*Tiruvāymoḻi*, Padikam 34 Stanza 8.

2. The names of half a dozen Pāṇḍyās of the *Puṟanāṉūṟu* period and those of an equal number of them taken from Mr. V. Venkayya's list compiled from the Vēḷvikuḍi grant of the 8th Century A. D. and the Madras Museum and Sinnamaṉūr plates, are appended here for comparison. They afford an interesting illustration of one of the many methods employed to utilize political power in furtherance of religion.

The Puṟanāṉūṟu Pāṇḍyas.	*The Later Pāṇḍyas.*
1. Ilavantikaippaḷḷi thuñchiya Nanmāṟan.	1. Māṟavarman Arikēsari Asamasaman.
2. Kūtākārathu thuñchiya Māṟan Vaḷuti	2. Kōchchaḍayan Raṇadhīran.
3. Chittira Māḍathu thuñchiya Nanmāṟan.	3. Arikēsari Parānkusa Māṟavarman Tērmāṟan.
4. Talaiyālaṅkānattu cheṟu venṟa Neḍumcheḻiyan.	4. Jaṭila Neḍunchaṭaya Parāntaka.
5. Veḷḷiyampalattu thuñchiya Peru Vaḷuti.	5. Srimāṟa Srivallabha Ēkavīra Parachakra Kōlāhaḷa, Pallavabhanjana.
6. Kānappēr tanta Ukkira Peru Vaḷuti.	6. Rājasimha Mandanagurava Abhimānamēru.

conciliate the kings and the masses alike proved, along with other causes like the advent of the religious devotees, the Nāyaṉmārs and the Āḷvārs, a powerful means of stamping out the Jaina and Buddhistic heterodoxy from the Tamil land in the course of the next few centuries. Among such devices of a later religious warfare, the Agastya tradition, as already observed, appears to be one. But it may still be asked why that tradition could not be given its face value and taken for one of the authentic race-lore of the Dravidians themselves. There is hardly any *a priori* necessity to dismiss such a supposition as unentertainable. Still the absolute silence of the entire Tamil Literature of the earliest period precludes us from considering it even as a reasonable historical hypothesis.

Predisposing causes for the acceptance of the Agastya tradition.

The most potent cause which appears to have predisposed the people to a ready acceptance of this foreign tradition was its appeal to the sense of racial dignity, or vanity perhaps, from which few races of antiquity are found to be free. If a sense of racial superiority is seen to persist even to this day among many enlightened people, one will not go wrong in positing its existence in those bygone times. At the beginning, the systematization, if not the creation, of the language of a people by some Divine agency or semi-divine sage must have evoked from them the greatest admiration and respect. And all the more powerful should be the influence of that doctrine when it puts their own language in a position of co-ordinate authority and odour of sanctity with the divine language of the North, the Sanskrit. Later literature is filled with allusions which express unfeigned gratification at the ennoblement of Tamil, to stand on a par with the sacred language of the Vēdas. Here are a few stanzas culled at random from some leading works:

1. " முத்தமிழு நான்மறையு மானான் கண்டாய் "

2. " செந்தமிழோ டாரியனைச் சீரியனை "

—திருநாவுக்கரசர் தேவாரம்.

3. " மந்தி போற்றிரிந் தாரி யத்தொடு செந்த மிழ்ப்பயன் தெரிகிலா
அந்த கர்க்கெளி யேன லேன்றிரு வாலவா யர னிற்கவே"

—திருஞானசம்பந்தர் தேவாரம்.

4. " விடையு கைத்தவன் பாணினிக் கிலக்கண மேனாள்
வடமொ ழிக்குரைத் தாங்கியன் மலயமா முனிக்குத்
திடமு றுத்தியம் மொழிக்கெதி ராக்கிய தென்சொல்
மடம கட்கரங் கென்பது வழுதிநா டன்றே."

—திருவிளையாடற்புராணம்.

5. " வடமொழியைப் பாணினிக்கு வகுத்தருளி யதற் கிணையாத்
தொடர்புடைய தென்மொழியை யுலகமெலாந் தொழு தேத்துங்
குடமுனிக்கு வலியுறுத்தார் கொல்லேற்றுப் பாகரெனின்
கடல்வரைப்பி னிதன்பெருமை யாவரே கணித்தறிவார்."

6. " இருமொழிக்குங் கண்ணுதலார் முதற்குரவ ரியல் வாய்ப்ப
இருமொழியும் வழிப்படுத்தார் முனிவேந்த ரிசைபரப்பும்
இருமொழியுந் தழீஇனா ரான்றவரே யென்றாலிவ்
விருமொழியு நிகரென்னு மிதற்கைய முளதேயோ."

—காஞ்சிபுராணம்.

7. " மறைமுதற் கிளந்த வாயான் மதிமுகிழ் முடித்த வேணி
யிறைவர்தம் பெயரை நாட்டி யிலக்கணஞ் செய்யப் பெற்றே

யறைகடல் வறைப்பிற் பாடை யனைத்தும்வென்
றாரியத்தோ
டுறழ்தரு தமிழ்த்தெய் வத்தை யுண்ணினைந் தேத்தல்
செய்வாம்."

—சீகாளத்திபுராணம்.

8. "தனிநடங் குயிற்றுஞ் சம்புநம் பெருமான்
றமருகப் பறைக்கண் அஇ உணு வென்
றமர்தரு சூத்திர மாதியீ ரேழ்பெறத்
திடமுற நன்கு தெரித்தமை போல
விந்தமும் வேலையு வீறுபோய்க் குன்றக்
கந்தமென் கமலக் கரத்தினை விதிர்த்து
அருந்தவக் கொள்கை யகத்திய முனிக்குத்
திருந்திசை நுணுக்கச் செந்தமி ழியலினைச்
செப்பினேன்"

—தாண்டவராய சுவாமிகள்.

These extracts, though made mostly from later authors, give us a valuable clue for correctly arriving at the motives that must have swayed the Tamil people in the ready acceptance of the Agastya legend.

Another predisposing cause might be drawn from the high character and religious sanctity of the few early Brahman settlers in the Tamil land. The arrival of the Aryans here must, in the ordinary course of events, have taken place only after the Mahārāṣṭra, Āndhra and Karnāṭaka countries had been fairly occupied by them. This penetration into the last two border countries of Tamiḻagam may require, at the lowest, two to three centuries from 350 B. C. So the first or the second century before Christ may reasonably be fixed as the *terminus a quo* beyond which the Aryan immigration into Tamiḻagam could not be pushed. That the Hindu Aryans who set foot in the Tamil land a little later hailed from these border countries receives some support from two subsequent traditions. One of this refers to Agastya bringing with him eighteen families of kings, Vēḷirs and Aruvāḷars from Tuvarāpati, the modern Dwārasamudram in the Mysore State, and the other to Paraśurāma peopling Kēraḷa[1] with colonists from the banks of the Godāvarī and the Krishṇā. The *Travancore State Manual* in page 213 refers to the latter tradition thus : "The new land was not fit for habitation ; the settling down had not been completed. The quaking did not cease, so the Purāṇa says : hence Paraśurāma sprinkled some gold dust and buried coins and thus formed a treasure-trove which stopped the quaking of the land. He prepared a great yāgam (Sacrifice) at Varkala for the same purpose. Thereafter Paraśurāma brought colonies of Brahmins from the north, from the banks of the Krishṇā, the Godāvarī, the Narmadā, the Kāverī and from Madura, Mysore and Māhārāṣṭra and from many other places and peopled Keralam. The Brahmin colonists so brought belonged to eight *gotrams* or families." Presumably this is a very late tradition. Still we may infer that what occurred in Kēraḷa has had its analogue in the Tamil land to the east of the ghats.[2] Larger and larger colonies of the Aryan immigrants must have come into the country from

---

1. Mr. Logan is of opinion that the Vedic Brahmans must have arrivad at Malabar in the early part of the 8th Century A. D., and not earlier and that they must have come from the coast of the Tuḷu country.

2. Is it not a little curious that identical methods have been adopted by the Āryan immigrants or their immediate descendants, in Peninsular India both in the East Coast and in the West? Agastya was brought into the Tamil country on the East Coast and Paraśurāma was planted on the West. Just as Paraśurāma created the whole Kēraḷam from out of the bed of the Arabian Sea and became its virtual proprietor, his Eastern companion seems to have got the whole Tamil country from God Skanda at Tiruvēṅkaṭam and handed it over to his Śiṣhya, the first Pāṇḍya king. Again as Paraśurāma had to people his new country by bringing down families of royalty and commonalty from the banks of the Godāvarī and the Krishṇā,

the watershed of the Krishṇā and the Godāvarī rivers, the Mahārāṣṭra and the Karnāṭaka in the West and of the Āndhra in the East. The picture presented by the earliest body of Tamil Literature, *viz.*, *Puṟanāṉūṟu*, *Akanāṉūṟu*, *Pattuppāṭṭu* etc., only tends to confirm the conclusion otherwise arrived at here. A few Brahman priests seem to have taken up their abode here and there and assisted the kings and chieftains in the performance of yāgas and other religious rites. Though they were very few in number, they had acquired by their learning, peaceful character and by their life of self-denial and high-aspiring spirituality an unbounded influence with the rulers and the ruled alike. The following quotations from *Puṟanāṉūṟu* will establish beyond doubt the sanctity that had already begun to hedge round the Brahman teachers of those days.[1]

Agastya had to take 18 families of kings, Vēḷirs and Aruvāḷars from Tuvarāpati (Dwārasamudram). The parallelism is not yet ended. Even as the West Coast owes its very rudiments of civilized life to Parasurāma, Agastya had also to perform his civilizing work by systematizing the Tamil Language and founding the first Academy whence all culture flowed for the benefit of later generations. After their labours for the spread of knowledge and culture, Parasurāma is said to have betaken himself to the Mahēndra Hill in Orissa, and Agastya, likewise, had to retire to the Pothiyil mount of the South. Just as Parasurāma who first reclaimed Śūrparaka country about Bombay in the North was later on shifted to the South to reclaim Kēraḷa, Agastya had to quit his Malakūṭa residence, in the Kanarese country, and take up his quarters in the Pothiyil mount in the heart of the Tamil country in the South. The inference from this close parallelism of traditions is obvious.

1. Mr. F. E. Pargiter, in his *Ancient Indian Historical Tradition*, p. 62, writes as follows: "There have been broadly speaking, three classes among Brahmins throughout Indian History, *viz.*, (1) The ascetic devotee and teacher, the ṛṣi or the

" இறைஞ்சுக பெருமநின் சென்னி சிறந்த
நான்மறை முனிவ ரேந்துகை யெதிரே "—6: Kārikiḻār.

" ஆவு மானியற் பார்ப்பன மாக்களும்"—9: Neṭṭimaiyār.

" பார்ப்பார்த் தப்பிய கொடுமை யோர்க்கும் "
—34: Ālattūrkkiḻār.

" * * * நின் முன்னோ ரெல்லாம்
பார்ப்பார் நோவன செய்யலர்",—43: Tāmappalkaṇṇaṉār.

This high respect, which the early Brahman priests won, naturally ripened in a few centuries into a blind belief on the part of the Tamilians in all the myths and legends which the ingenuity of the priestly order could coin for success in a life-and-death grapple with the heretics.

---

muni ; (2) priest and the spiritual guide of Kings, nobles and people ; and (3) the minister of State, Royal Officer and those who followed secular employments. The first was the Brahman *par excellence*, the Saint ; the second the priest and the preceptor ; and the third the semi-secular Brahman and sometimes wholly a layman." In the Tamil country the earliest Brahman settlers as testified to by literature seem to have belonged to the second class mentioned by Mr. Pargiter. Except Agastya, Tamil land cannot boast of a single Aryan Rishi as having had his hermitage within its borders. Living secluded in their forest hermitages, and cut off from the current of secular life, those Aryan Rishis did not come to the South. The later Tamil Purāṇic writers, for their own purposes, had to draw their Rishis from the Naimisa and other forests in North India. This total absence of the Aryan Rishi or his hermitage in the Tamil land renders Agastya's connection with the South highly problematical, being a solitary exception which does not fit in with historic conditions and chronology. Aryan immigration into the Tamil land in any considerable scale having begun in the Post-Christian centuries, the attempt to import therein a Rishi belonging to the Pre-Christian period is nothing less than a crude anachronism.

And a third predisposing cause arises from the decadence which the Tamilians fell into after attaining the elements of a material civilization so clearly reflected in what is admittedly the classical portion of Tamil Literature. A period of repose, as in the case of other nations, followed in the wake of one of constructive and creative activity and the national mind then appears to have fallen into a torpor. Here too, as elsewhere, idle minds fell a prey to superstition—for a serious active life and superstition never go together—and when this superstition entered into alliance with religion, human nature could not but succumb.

The mystery of the religion of *Nāṉmaṟai*, the four sealed arcana, and the miracles of devotees and religious preachers will, as a matter of course, make a powerful appeal to the masses whose minds have already grown vacant by a life of enervating ease and inactivity. It is difficult to imagine how the successors of the early Tamilians who had achieved such wonderful success in many of the arts of civilized life at so early an age could have allowed themselves to be thus hopelessly bound by the mythologic cobwebs of a later time. The mystery of this will vanish the moment we realise that human nature—even the best cultivated—can in no way be developed all-round. Its strength in one direction spells weakness in another. This is the Nemesis that always dogs the footsteps of every specialist. If he is great in one field, he must pay the penalty by his weakness in another. The practical Tamil intellect, when it had accomplished its work of building up a material civilization and felt itself flagged, was only too ready to receive its spiritual pabulum and mythologic luxuries from the Aryans of the North.

Agastya tradition in the Ramayana.

Not only is the Agastya tradition a late one in the Tamil land, its earliest reference in the Rāmāyaṇa of Vālmīki comes to us with a clear impress of an inherent contradiction. Rāma first meets Agastya, as I stated before, at his āśram near Nāsik and under the direction of the latter takes up his residence at Pañcavaṭī. It was here that the abduction of Sītā by Rāvaṇa takes place and thereafter Rāma moves southward to Kiṣkindhā and enters into an alliance with Sugrīva, the monkey-chief. In the course of the instructions to the search-parties despatched by Sugrīva for finding out Sītā, a somewhat minute geographical description of South India is given to Hanumān, who had been chosen with Aṅgada to lead the southern party. In this occurs a reference to the sandalwooded Malaya to the south of the river Kāvēri as the seat of the famous Saint Agastya. A modern reader of the Rāmāyaṇa must feel considerable perplexity in reconciling the existence of the sage just a few yojanas to the north of the Pañcavaṭī with his residence at Pothiyil, a distance of more than 800 miles to the south. This obvious inconsistency could be got over only by assuming that the mention of Agastya's residence in the southern mountain was a subsequent interpolation made by one who had more knowledge of South India, especially of the Tamil Kingdoms in the south, than Vālmīki himself who mentions the southern ocean as lying just a few yojanas off from the foot of the Vindhya mountains. Supernaturalists may credit the sage with powers of swift locomotion through the air and may not feel puzzled how the sage could live about the Vindhya mountains in the north and in a short time find himself seated in the Malaya Hills of the far-distant south.

But that hypothesis will not suit the demands of sober history. Hence we have to conclude that the testimony of the *Rāmāyaṇa* which has been undergoing numerous redactions till the first century B.C. or even later,[1] does in no way enable us to argue for a high antiquity for this tradition in Tamiḻagam.

Taking along with this the complete silence of the Tamil classical literature spread about the first three centuries of the Christian Era, the conclusion appears highly probable that the fourth, fifth and sixth centuries after Christ, which mark the keenest struggle with the heretical sects in the Tamil Land, may also have been the period when the first seeds of the Agastya tradition were sown in the South. How entirely incorrect is the surmise of Dr. Caldwell who claimed for the tradition an antiquity going back to 700 B. C. needs therefore no further elucidation.

Agastya Tradition and Tolkappiyam.

Conceding for the present that the poets who composed the works which are generally known as "Sangam Literature" may have omitted to make mention of Agastya for various reasons of their own, still we shall be precluded from making such a concession in the case of Tolkāppiyar, his leading disciple, and the author of the first and foremost Grammar of the Tamil Language. It is quite reasonable to expect that at least he, considering his relationship with the sage and by the special fact of his composing a grammar to compete with the monumental work of his master, should have given us some information regarding his reputed predecessor. Has he done anything of the kind ? Not a line is there in all that extent of his great grammar which may be construed even as an indirect reference to the Sage.[2] Tradition, whose

---

1. For instance, Dr. Washburne Hopkins in his work, the *Great Epic of India* fixes 400 A.D. as the latest date.

2. It is true that Nachchinārkkiniyar interprets certain sūtras of *Tolkāppiam* ending in என்ப, மொழிப, etc., whose reference is not at all specific as a reference by implication to Agastya, the author's guru. But the correct method of interpreting these indefinite statements of Tolkāppiyar is to be drawn

origin though late remains obscure, is no doubt responsible for creating twelve disciples who had to sit at the feet of Agastya for their learning. They were (1) Tiraṉadhūmākkini *alias* Tolkāppiyar ; (2) Chempūṭchēy ; (3) Ataṅkōṭṭācāṉ ; (4) Turāliṅkaṉ ; (5) Vāiyāppikaṉ ; (6) Vāyppiyaṉ ; (7) Paṉampāraṉ ; (8) Kaḻāramban ; (9) Avinayaṉ ; (10) Kakkaipāṭiniyaṉ ; (11) Naṟṟattaṉ and Vāmanaṉ. Sometimes Sikanṭi is seen interpolated in the list. It is worthy of note that Paṉampāraṉar, one of the co-students who studied with Tolkāppiyar at the Agastya Academy, is credited with composing an introductory stanza for his mate's work *Tolkāppiyam*. Here a reference is made to Ataṅkōṭṭācāṉ, another class-mate of theirs, and also to Tolkāppiyar's proficiency in the Aindra School of Sanskrit Grammar. Here too, Agastya has been passed over in studied silence. Even assuming that Tolkāppiyar's relationship with Agastya was a trifle strained—as Tradition assures us—there is not the slightest ground why Paṉampāraṉār should forget his guru in this recommendatory stanza. Not only has the sage been severely left out in the cold, but to add insult to injury Paṉampāraṉār makes another of their co-students, Ataṅkōṭṭācāṉ, preside over the assembly which had gathered to hear the exposition of Tolkāppiyar's great work and set on it its seal of approval. Is it conceivable that these three students of Agastya would have behaved so indecorously as they seem to have done, if they had actually acknowledged the great sage as their preceptor? The conduct of this student-triumvirate is explicable only on the assumption that none of them had anything to do with Agastya and might be

---

from certain other sūtras of that author which contain wordings like 'நுண்ணிதி னுணர்ந்தோர் கண்டவாறே,' 'என்மனார் புலமையோரே,' 'என்ப உணருமோரே,' 'என்ப அறிந்திசினோரே.' Explicitly and quite decisively these refer only to previous grammarians in general and not to Agastya in particular.

supposed to have been even ignorant of his very existence at the time. The perversity, which undoubtedly seems to cling to their conduct in this matter, is entirely due to our trying to foist on them a later day legend, for which they could hardly be called to account. If, however, we dismiss the Agastya legend as a piece of chronological irrelevancy, the conduct of Tolkāppiyar, Paṉampāraṉār and Ataṅkōṭṭācāṉ assumes quite a natural character.

Agastya's Works.

Tradition credits Agastya with founding the first Sangam and presiding over it. He is also represented as having composed the first Grammar of the Tamil Language. The Sangam tradition, as it stands, is too indefinite and etherial to be made the subject-matter of any historical investigation; for it does not afford us anywhere any foothold, any solid verifiable fact, from which to start. Nearly the whole body of it hangs in cloudland and few will be disposed to tamper with that beautiful aerial structure with prosaic confrontation with facts and historical deductions. Scientific criticism must feel a little nonplussed when vast periods of geological time are allowed to step into the limited field of a nation's literary history. Nor do the later Noachian Deluge and Manu's flood offer us a surer ground to plant ourselves on.[1] So, the Sangam

---

1. Regarding such deluges Mr. L. W. King writes thus in page 121 of his work *Babylonian Religion and Mythology.*

"In the tradition of many races scattered in various parts of the world is to be found a story, under many different forms and with many variations, of a great flood or deluge which in former times inundated and laid waste the land in which they dwelt. The explanation that such traditions refer to a universal deluge which took place in the early ages of the world, is now generally regarded as inadmissible, inasmuch as there is no trace of such a catastrophe in the earth's geological formation. Moreover Science has shown that in the present physical condition of the world such a universal deluge would be impossible."

question may be left undisturbed for the present.[1]

Agastya's composition of the first Tamil Grammar, however, stands on a different footing. It opens for us an avenue of approach. Though here also, according to tradition, the major portion of his work is said to have fallen into the maws of a far-distant time, still some stray sūtras of his have escaped that fate and come down to us. These, then, should give us some interesting materials for judging, however imperfectly, the nature of Agastya's extensive grammar of twelve thousand sūtras

---

1. It is worthy of note, in this connection, that no champion of the Sangam has yet come forward to seriously refute any of the arguments contained in the searching criticism of the late Prof. Seshagiri Sastri on the subject. The attempt of the late Prof. P. Sundaram Pillai, who ingeniously put forward the best defence the question admitted of, that the Sangam poets though belonging to various times and places were brought together in a group because in the historical perspective of a distant posterity they appeared to hang together, is really giving away the whole case. No doubt, it is a poetic way of defending the Sangam ; but the historic authenticity of the latter must be built upon more solid materials than figurative language. So the arguments of Prof. Seshagiri Sastri still hold the field. The mistaken impression that the antiquity of Tamil Literature has to be surrendered in the absence of a Sangam to support it from behind has been at the root of this tradition being carefully preserved, tended and made to persist even now. The earliest Tamil works—the Sangam literature—have undoubted intrinsic merits of their own and carry with them their own credentials for the grateful acceptance of the present-day Tamilian. Instead of establishing their antiquity on these intrinsic historic grounds, as I think we can very well do, some are engaged in propping it up on such extrinsic and almost legendary data as the three Sangams. In my view, it is certainly spoiling a strong case by unnecessary mythologizing.

and of the grain and temper of scholarship that characterised its author.

Before we proceed to value the fragments of Agastya's Grammar which have been handed down by the Tamil commentators and collected by a recent editor, it will not be out of place to glance incidentally at the huge body of miscellaneous writings which has since been ascribed to him. They range over a wide field from Medicine and Mysticism to Magic and Witchcraft[1] and bear eloquent testimony to their author having been an unabashed charlatan. The reputed systematiser of the Tamil Language could scarcely have descended so low as to produce such senseless and dismal drivel as the extant Agastya literature, which has absolutely nothing in either matter or form to commend it to a cultured society. This is what Professor Mahāmahopādhyāya S. Kuppuswami Sastriar, M. A., says in the introduction to Part II of Vol. II of the Descriptive Catalogue of the Oriental Manuscripts Library, Madras: "The name of Agastya or Ahattiyar in Tamil has to be specially mentioned as the most prolific writer on these subjects (Alchemy, Medicine, Yogam of the Siddhars). Who this Agastiyar is. to whom so many works are attributed, cannot be stated. He does not seem to be the same as the well-known Agastiyar, who is said to have systematized the Tamil Language and wrote the First Tamil Grammar. In all probability works written by

---

1. The Catalogue of the Madras Oriental Manuscripts Library gives, in all, details of about 96 Agastya works. May be this collection just touches only the fringe of a body of literature not yet fully explored. If the cavernous profundity of that author could gush forth in such numbers as

"பாரப்பா வாதத்தில் லக்ஷம் காப்புப்
பாடினேன் வைத்தியத்தில் ரெண்டு லெக்ஷம்"

could even the most conscientious book-collector ever think of running the whole quarry to earth?

different persons at different periods of time seem to have been attributed to Ahattiyar to invest them with dignity and antiquity, but the language used in many of these works is very commonplace and betrays them in their true colour as later compositions." To call the language of this trashy collection—for literature is too dignified a name to be used for it—'commonplace' is to err on the side of moderation. Let me extract a few lines of verse for the judgment of the reader.

"சேதியொன்று சொல்லுகிறேன் தெளிவாய்க் கேளு
செகந்தனிலே சாமளா தேவி தன்னை"

—ஊழிக்காற்றுச் சூத்திரம்

"சாமிந்தப் பூரணத்தைக் கெணியா தீந்தால்
தலைதெறித்துப் போகுமடா சத்தியஞ் சொன்னேன்"

—அகத்தியர் பூரணசூத்திரம் இருநூற்றுப்பதினாறு

"வெளியாகச் சூத்திரத்தை வெளி விடாதே
வேதாந்தப் புத்தியினால் நூலைக் காரு"

—அகத்தியர் கலைஞான சூத்திரம் ஆயிரத்து இருநூறு

"வித்தையென்ற வித்தையெல்லாம் நூற்றுக் குள்ளே
விருதிட்டு வெட்டுதற்கு சுழுகு"

—அகத்தியர் வைத்தியநூறு

"சுழியான அகரமே உகர மாச்சு
சூட்சமாய் எழுத்தெல்லா மிதனா லாச்சு"

—அகத்தியர் எட்டு

"சஞ்சீவி போலிந்த நூலைச் சொன்னோம்
 சண்டாளப் பாவிகளுக் கீய வேண்டாம்
நஞ்சுபோ லிந்தமுறை நாய்களுக்கு
 நலமான நாய்களைத் தானாகக் கொல்லும்
கெஞ்சுவார் உலகத்தா ரிந்த நூலை
 கேட்டாலுங் கொடுக்கரிது கேள்வி யின்றி
மிஞ்சவே பஞ்சரித்து தெண்டன் செய்து
 வேணதனை மீய்ந்தக்கா லிதனை ஈயே."

—அகத்தியர் சூத்திரம் இருநூற்றுப்பத்து

Is this 'commonplace' language or the language of puny minds absolutely devoid of learning, culture, and moral elevation? The Professor is again a little cautious and hesitating to draw the conclusion that the whole lot bears the impress of the popular mint of quite recent times. Such lines as:

"வானைத் தாவிய பொதிகை தன்னில்வாழ்
மகத்தான ரிஷியுடைய வாக்கு நேர்மை"

—அகத்தியர் தீக்ஷாவிதி

"எத்திடு சன்னிதோஷம் எழுப்பிடும் குஷ்டரோகம்
போற்றிடு நீருமென்றே பொருப்புமே விருந்தோர்
சொன்னார்"

—அகத்தியர் வைத்தியம்பதினறு

occurring in some of the works themselves give the lie direct to their ever having been written by the sage himself. But why waste time in exploring the back alleys and slums of Tamil Literature?

In retracing his steps to the grammatical sūtras of Agastya, the reader may expect that perhaps in these the reputed sage might be seen at his best. But I fear blank disappointment must greet him here also. First, a few specimens of the sūtras of this far-famed originator of the first Tamil Grammar. His definitions of E<u>l</u>uttu (எழுத்து) Mo<u>l</u>i (மொழி) and Kū<u>r</u><u>r</u>u (கூற்று) are illuminating to the last degree and we feel that without his critical guidance in a region so recondite we would be left in the lurch for ever.

எழுத்து

"எழுதப் படுதலா லெழுத்தெனப் பெயர்பெறும்."

மொழி

"மொழிந்த வெழுத்தான் மொழிவதே மொழியாம்."

கூற்று

"கூறு படுத்தலால் கூற்றெனப்படும்."

Then he gives the lead to future grammarians how they should distinguish between the sexes of letters :

"குறிலாண் பாலு நெடில்பெண் பாலுமாம்"
"ஆயுதமும் மெய்யு மலியெனப் படுமே"

His medical knowledge is perhaps responsible for another peculiar classification of letters or sounds into Amirtaveḻuttu (அமிர்தவெழுத்து) and Nañceḻuttu (நஞ்செழுத்து). His intuitive apprehension of the individuality of the Tamil Language comes out in the Sūtra :

“ஐந்தொழி யெழுத்தெலாம் வடவெழுத் தாகும்”

This solitary Sūtra is enough to blow up the patriotic pretensions of the so-called Tamil Muni? Probably, Agastya, a foreigner in the Tamil land, had a better justification for claiming the ownership of even primary human sounds to the Sanskrit Language, than the bigoted author of *Ilakkaṇakkottu* (இலக்கணக்கொத்து) of modern days in perpetrating that absurd violation of the most elementary conceptions of linguistic science. The tell-tale sūtras, I here extract, from the published volume of Rao Saheb Bhavanandam Pillai's edition of *Pērakattiya Tiraṭṭu*, will not fail to impress the reader with their brand-new modernity. If the words, style and thoughts of a literary composition can furnish the critic with any standard for fixing its date with some approach to tolerable accuracy, the following sūtras can lead but to one conclusion. They are all post-Tolkāppiyam in origin and bear evident marks of pedantry in some and of grammatical dilettantism in others. Here are the Sūtras :

Sutra :

4. இரேகை வரிபொறி யிலேகையக் கரப்பெயர்.
10. அச்சாவி சுரம்பூத மாமுயிரின் பெயர்.
13. குறிலுங் குறுமையு மிரச்சுவமுங் குறிற்பெயர்.
15. நெடிலும் நெடுமையுந் தீர்க்கமு நெடிற்பெயர்.
27. உடலுடம் பொற்றல் லூமைவியஞ் சனமெய்.
31. வலிவன்மை வன்கணம் பரிசம்வல் லினப்பெயர்.
61. ஆத னநாதியு முதாநறு தியுமா
நாதமுரங் கண்டந் தலையிட முற்றும்
பல்லிதழ் 'நாமூக் கணைமைந் தொழிலா
வெல்லா வெழுத்தும் பிறக்கு மென்ப.
78. தலைமையக் கரம்போல் சார்பெழுத் தற்பவம்.

89. மயக்கம் புணர்ச்சி சங்கமஞ் சையோகங்
கூடல் கலத்தல் புல்லலொரு பொருட்சொலே.
139. தனிமொழி யிணைமொழி துணைமொழி பொதுமொழி
கணமொழி தணமொழி கலப்புறு மொழியேழ்.
141. சநுக்கிரகஞ் சங்கத மவப்பிரஞ்சநம் பாகதம்
மொழிநான் கென்றே மொழியப் படுமே.
142. சநுக்கிரகஞ் சங்கதந் தேவர்மொழி யென்ப.
143. அவப்பிரஞ் சநமொழி யசேதனர்க் காகும்.
144. எல்லர் நாட்டிலு மியல்வது பாகதம்.
145. பாகதம், தற்பவந் தற்சமந் தேசிய மெனப்படும்.
148. தேசியந் திசைச்சொ லென்று செப்புக.
149. தீர்க்கங் குணம் விருத்தி சந்தி மூவகையாம்.
163. எயன் விகுதி யெய்தும் பிள்ளைக்கே.

எழியன் முறைய தெதிர்முக வேற்றுமை
வேறென விளம்பான் பெயரது விகாரமென்
றோதிய புலவனு[1] முளனொரு வகையா
னிந்திர னெட்டாம் வேற்றுமை யென்றனன்.
—பேரகத்திய மேற்கோட் சூத்திரம், 14

It is hardly doubtful whether the author or authors of such miscellanea had any clear notions of the function and scope of Grammar and Lexicology. The conceptions of these two disciplines are so hopelessly mixed up in these. Next, the style and phraseology of the Sūtras have neither simplicity nor ancientness about them. Both point unmistakably to the very latest period in the growth of grammatical terminology. In the third place, the attempt to squeeze the classification and nomenclature of the Sanskrit Grammarians into the facts of an alien language is only too patent throughout. The author of *Tolkāppiyam*, in spite of his Sanskrit erudition, had at least the sound instinct of a born grammarian to respect

---

1. This clearly referring to Pāṇini, Agastya must be considered as having lived after him. How could the Ṛg Vēdic Agastya come after Pāṇini ?

the linguistic phenomena of a foreign tongue and to carefully avoid tampering with their peculiarities in his classical grammar. Later-day scholars, in their admiration of Sanskrit, seem to have been engaged in importing wholesale the conceptions and terminology of the Sanskrit Grammarians in the form of stray sūtras composed for the nonce and fathering them on the great saint Agastya with a view to secure for their productions an authority more ancient and compelling than what belongs to *Tolkāppiyam.*

Agastya Sutras and Tolkappiyam.

In the light of the exuberance of this orthodox Tamil Literature, the hypothesis of *Tolkāppiyam* being the work of an early Jaina author can scarcely be lightly brushed aside[1]. The difficulty, however, of coming to any

1. The identification of Tolkāppiyar with Tṛṇadhūmāgni, the son of Jamadagni, the Vēdic Ṛṣī, is due to a later tradition and is absolutely indefensible on historical grounds. To assign *Tolkāppiyam* to the fourth century A. D. is indeed a reasonable working hypothesis and this receives extraneous support from the facts of Tamil Literary development also. If however, the Vēdic Ṛṣī, Jamadagni, the father of Parasurāma and of Tṛṇadhūmāgni, is imported into the story of this work, the whole ends in a chronological dislocation of no ordinary kind. That Jamadagni lived towards the close of the Kṛta Age is the view of the Purāṇas. Summing up their conclusions, Mr. F. E. Pargiter writes, in page 315 of his *Ancient Indian Historical Tradition* thus :—" According to that reckoning Viswāmitra and his sons (with whom began the real Vedic Age, as mentioned above) lived towards the close of the Kṛta Age and so also Jamadagni etc." The following observations of Dr. Burnell are apposite in this connection : " It is possible to show historically how the Brahman gradually supplanted the old Buddhist-Jaina civilization of the Peninsula, the earliest historical civilization of which there is any record in that part of India ; and the fact that the Vedas of the South are the same as those of the North proves conclusively that this was done at a time when the Brāhmaṇas and the Sūtras had been definitely reduced to

definite conclusion on that question arises from the fact that the theological conceptions and cosmogonic legends of the Jainas show a family likeness to those of the orthodox Hindus except in a few abstract doctrinal points.[1] There is reason for believing that the Agastya mint was opened and kept going for sometime solely to bring down the authority of *Tolkāppiyam* and belittle its importance. Viewed in its historical setting, Agastya tradition appears as little else than an orthodox counter-blast to *Tolkāppiyam.* But the superior merits of that work could not thus be extinguished. It stood its ground and even at this distance of time while a number of grammatical works have in the interim succeeded it, its broadly-laid foundations have not been touched nor the classic brilliance of its superstructure surpassed. Thus

---

their present form or at all events not before the Christian Era."—*Elements of South Indian Palaeography, pp.* 11—12.

Prof. E. J. Rapson in page 66 of his work *Ancient India* says " They (the Jains) have also played a notable part in the civilization of Southern India, where the early literary development of the Kanarese and Tamil Languages was due, in a great measure, to the labours of Jain monks."

1. This may be also due to the wonderful assimilative capacity of the Hindu Religion, which has always received into its bosom alien doctrines, admitted into its pantheon alien gods and thrown open the doors of its hagiology to alien religious teachers. The admission of Buddha, the stoutest and the most formidable opponent of Brahmanism, into the Hindu circle of Avatārs is alone sufficient to establish the great catholicity of Hinduism. The remarkable strength of this religion is no doubt partly due to this.

That the same tendency was powerfully at work in the heterodox sects too need not be doubted. The following observation of Mr. Vincent A. Smith applies with double force to the Jaina sect : " The newer form of Buddhism had much in common with older Hinduism and the relation is so close that even an expert often feels a difficulty in deciding to which

there is ample justification for concluding that the Agastya tradition is decidedly posterior to the early Jaina period[1] of Tamil Literature, and must be ascribed to the age which succeeded the composition of *Tolkāppiyam*. Another ground of improbability of the so-called *Agastyam* being anterior to *Tolkāppiyam* may also be adverted to here. If the original grammar, *Agastyam*, had really treated of the three kinds of Tamil, *viz.*, *Iyal*, *Icai*, and *Nāṭakam*, there was hardly any reason for Tolkāppiyar to omit the treatment of *Icai* and *Nāṭakam* in his great work. He too would have followed his predecessor and given his grammar an all-comprehensiveness which, at present, it lacks. His failure to do so was due simply to the fact that the tripartite classification of Tamil into *Iyal*, *Icai* and *Nāṭakam* did not exist in his time. It was introduced only at a later stage of the growth of the Tamil Language and stamps *Agastyam* as a work of that period.

Agastya Sutras—A Later Forgery.

The time and circumstances of the origin of Agastya sūtras, no less than their language and import, are such as will warrant only one conclusion, that the whole mass of them is a bare-faced forgery—not, of course, committed by a single writer at a single period of time but the result of different authors at diverse times contributing their share to the pile, whose sundry fragments challenge our

---

system a particular image should be assigned."—*Early History of India*, p. 319.

Compare also Mr. Vincent A. Smith's views in the same work *re* the absorption of foreign elements into the Hindu Society, given in pages 340 and 341 and the decay of Buddhism in India, in p. 382.

1. 'The age of Tiruñānasambandha and Tirunāvukkarasu, about the beginning of the 7th century A. D. may be taken as the dividing line which marks the earlier and the later periods of the Jain History in Tamiḻagam. . . . . .

attention to-day and create a problem in the linguistic and literary history of Tamil for solution. That this is not mere idle theorizing will come home to the reader if he has the patience to scrutinize a little the language of the following Agastya sūtras extracted from the commentaries of Naccinārkkiniyar on *Jīvaka-Cintāmaṇi* and of Aṭiyārk-kunallār on *Cilappatikāram.*

1. " சாந்திக் கூத்தும் விநோதக் கூத்துமென்
றாய்ந்துற வகுத்தன னகத்தியன் றானே."
2. "எழுவகைக் கூத்து மிழிகுலத் தோரை
யாட வகுத்தன னகத்தியன் றானே."
3. தக்கராக நோதிறங் காந்தாரம் பஞ்சமமே
துக்கங் கழிசோம ராகமே—மிக்கதிறற்
காந்தார மென்றைந்தும் பாலைத் திறமென்றார்
பூந்தா ரகத்தியனார் போந்து".

Is it unfair to suppose that these late commentators, who quote such sūtras without letting us know whence they drew them, should have really intended that they should be taken for Agastya sūtras ? If Agastya were the real author, why should he have referred to himself at all and that also in the third person ? Surely, one will find it difficult to ascribe such vanity, as this language pre-supposes, to a Sage of Agastya's saintliness and eminence. The only way then of explaining away what to us looks like effrontery is to conclude that these are not the genuine writings of Agastya but only forgeries perpetrated by the later devotees of the Agastya cult. The reference to these sūtras in the commentaries does in no way establish their authenticity. On the other hand, they are rendered doubly suspicious, first by the suppression of the names of their authors and secondly by the absence of the original Agastya sūtras on which these later ones might be supposed to have been based. Hence this floatsam and jetsam of Agastya Literature deserves only to be stored away in a special niche reserved for literary forgeries until their authenticity is vouched for by extraneous evidence of an incontrovertible kind.

Agastya Tradition in Later Tamil Literature.

Human mind loves the marvellous. Even now it has not clean outgrown that habit. When once the Agastya Tradition was planted in the Tamil soil, it burst into a rank and over-abundant growth. The following quotations from certain later Tamil works will bear this out.

Pannirupaṭalam has the following in its *Pāyiram*:

" வீங்குகட லுடுத்த வியன்கண் ஞாலத்துத்
தாங்கா நல்லிசைத் தமிழ்க்குவிளக் காகென
வானோ ரேத்தும் வாய்மொழிப் பல்புகழ்
ஆனாப் பெருமை அகத்திய னென்னும்
அருந்தவ முனிவ னாக்கிய முதனூல்
பொருந்தக் கற்றுப் புரைதப வுணர்ந்தோர்
நல்லிசை நிறுத்த தொல்காப்பியன்."

The *Pāyiram* of *Puṟapporuḷ Veṇpā Mālai* contains this :

" மன்னிய சிறப்பின் வானோர் வேண்டத்
தென்மலை யிருந்த சீர்சால் முனிவரன்
றன்பாற் றண்டமிழ் தாவின் றுணர்ந்த
துன்னருஞ் சீர்த்தித் தொல்காப் பியன்."

The *Pāyiram* of *Akapporuḷ Viḷakkam* runs thus :

" பூமலி நாவன் மாமலைச் சென்னி
ஈண்டிய விமையோர் வேண்டலிற் போந்து
குடங்கையின் விந்த நெடுங்கிரி மிசைதீர்த்
தலைகட லடக்கி மலயத் திருந்த
இருந்தவன் றன்பா லியற்றமி ழுணர்ந்த
புலவர் பன் னிருவருட் டலைவ னாகிய
தொல்காப்பியன்."

The *Divākaram* has the following :

" வருநற் கங்கை வடதிசைப் பெருமையுந்
தென்றிசைச் சிறுமையு நீக்கிய குறுமுனி

குண்டிகைப் பழம்புனற் காவிரிப் பெரும்பதி
யம்பற்கதிபதி."

These references are enough to establish how the Agastya tradition first began in the upper stratum of Tamil Literature before trickling down to its lower or the popular level.

Agastya Tradition in Tamil Puranic Literature.

Leaving these, if we turn to Tamil Purāṇic Literature of still later times, the Agastya legend will be found to have grown in extent and elaborateness, which the earlier writers could hardly have even imagined. The first promulgators of the Purāṇas in the Tamil land being Poets, the characters and incidents of North Indian Traditions were imported bodily into their works and handled with a freedom which the imaginative children of Poetry alone possess. Kantapurāṇam (*a*), Kācikāṇṭam (*b*), Tirukkuṟṟālappurāṇam (*c*), Tiruvēṅkaṭattalappurāṇam (*d*), Tirunelvēlittalappurāṇam (*e*), Kuṭantaippurāṇam (*f*), Mayilaippurāṇam (*g*), Vētāraṇiyappurāṇam (*h*), [1] to mention only a few, have each something to say about the saint and his miraculous performances. The array of the Purāṇic battalion is indeed tremendous, but its arms are loaded with only blank cartridges. It may envelop itself in vast volumes of smoke and rattle ; but for hitting at one fact of history it has not the means. Still some people feel a sort

---

1. (*a*) *vide* அகத்தியப்படலம்.
   (*b*) ,, திருமணச்சருக்கம்.
   (*c*) ,, தேவர்கள் அகத்தியாசிரமமடைந்த சருக்கம்.
   (*d*) ,, அகத்தியர் திருமலை வலம்வந்த அத்தியாயம்.
   (*e*) ,, விந்தகிரிச் சருக்கம்.
   (*f*) ,, p. 198.
   (*g*) ,, பொதியமாமலைச் சருக்கம் ; தலவிசிட்டச் சருக்கம்.
   (*h*) ,, மணவாளக்கோலச் சருக்கம்.

of unctuous over-scrupulousness of spirit and refrain from rejecting these myths of the poets as utterly worthless for historic purposes. Emulating the example of historians who try to extract some grains of truth from ancient traditions, they go on to argue whether the testimony of such a goodly company of Purāṇic poets should not after all have some bed-rock of truth underneath. This is entirely misconceiving the problem that has been set forth in this paper and the method adopted for its solution. Inductive methods, which, when applied to facts, are a fruitful source of truth, will yield only fictitious generalizations when applied to fictions. There is no intrinsic merit in these scientific methods to impart to the materials to which they are applied the validity of truth that they may otherwise lack. It is surprising that this commonplace of scientific doctrine and practice is forgotten by those who want to appeal to the testimony of numbers, where each number counted is little better than a zero. Surely, the false concurrent statement of a hundred unveracious witnesses will not make that statement true simply because their number happens to be hundred. On the method of inductive reasoning these adopt, almost every character of every poet and mythologist must be credited with real existence. Would Shakespeare have treated the history of Falstaff in three successive plays of his, if there had not been some real Falstaff to become the hero of so many exploits and escapades ? How, for instance, could the numerous adventures and hairbreadth escapes of the great detective hero, Sherlock Holmes, be made consistent with his assumed non-existence? The numerous exploits of those two heroes should force us to conclude that, discounting much as due to poetic fancy or a novelist's imagination, there must still remain a nucleus of solid fact at the core. A reasoning like this is not at all different in essentials from that which guides certain investigators in their work of constructing history with the help of the Purāṇic poets. The attempts of these remind us of the venerable Professors of the University of Lagado, who were engaged in grim earnest in extracting sunbeams from cucumbers.

Apotheosis of Agastya.

When Agastya passed from the hands of the Poets to the care of the masses, his saintliness came to be immediately surrounded with a halo of divinity. In all countries and at all times, group psychology has been characterised by one feature—its tendency to occupy extremes either way.[1] Hence, measured judgments, appreciation within limits, are not of the people. They must make of the persons brought to their bar either a god or a devil. Naturally, therefore, the popular Agastya was raised at once to the rank of a divinity and their worshipful homage flowed towards him in an unceasing stream. A temple too, known as Agastīśvaram, was raised in his honour and it stands to this day some four or five miles to the north of Cape Comorin. Though this temple has now fallen into neglect, it must have at one time attracted a large concourse of votaries and been an important

---

1. "It is the lack of the conditions necessary to collective resolution and volition that renders a crowd so fickle and so inconsistent ; so capable of passing from one extreme of action to another, of hurrying to death the man whom it glorified at an earlier moment, or of turning from savage butchery to tender and tearful solicitude."—William McDougall's '*Group Mind*' p. 45. Just as the lack of the conditions necessary to collective resolution leads to the fickleness of the crowd, so also the want of facilities for collective deliberation and judgment of the populace precludes the application of the necessary corrective and brings about the extremist character of popular judgments in general.

place of pilgrimage. That Agastīśvaram may have once enjoyed its heyday of prosperity is rendered probable by the fact that the Taluq or revenue division in which it is located is even now known as Agastīśvaram Taluq in South Travancore.[1] Not only this, there are certain communities in that part of the country, the weaving class for instance, who consider the saint as their own tribal deity and offer him regular daily worship.

Another religious cult also later on seems to have mingled itself with the Agastya. When the Śaivite religious philosophers appeared and began to spiritualize still more the religious conceptions of the earlier Nāyaṉmārs in South India, they depicted God as the spiritual guru who would present himself before devout and ripe souls and free them from the coils of Karma and rebirth by bestowing *mukti* on them. This special grace on the part of Śiva, the Supreme Lord, became one of the cardinal doctrines of the Śaiva Siddhānta School of Philosophy, which even now claims the largest number of adherents in South India. That Śaivism, at least in its latest phase, emphasising as it did *Guru-Bhakti* as the foremost virtue amongst its three types of spiritual devotion, powerfully reacted on the Agastya cult and helped its spread amongst the masses goes without saying. An ācārya of the type of Agastya, hovering midway between Divinity and man, could very easily be taken for Śiva. Guru or the divine teacher himself. And in fact no orthodox Śaivite could afford to treat a religious guru with indifferent feelings lest he should thereby lose the chance of salvation, which would be vouchsafed to him

1. There is a village known as Tiru-Agattiyānpaḷḷi, about two miles to the south of Tirumaṟaikkāṭu, in the Tanjore District. The Saint is said to have performed penance here for some time. This place comes within the itinerary of the Śaiva devotee Tiruñānasambandha and is found mentioned in one of his hymns

by Śiva himself appearing in the form of a human teacher, at some time or other. Thus, in the identification of the Saint with Śiva Guru Mūrttam, brought about by the exigencies of Śaivite religious development, the apotheosis of Agastya reaches its finale in the Tamil land.

The following details given in Mr. Gangoly's article in the *Journal of the Mythic Society* throw a fresh light on an earlier phase of the same religious tendency working itself out in the Malay islands in the East. In Java certain images called "Śiva Guru" or "Triśūla" images are found in many places and are worshipped as those of Agastya, who is believed to have been the first missionary of Śaivism in that country. This, in a way, explains how in the mainland of India Agastya cult received a fresh impetus by its alliance with the Śaiva revivalism, especially during its later stages when its doctrines and rituals were elaborated and codified by Meykaṇṭa Tēva and the other religious philosophers who followed him. That of all teachers Agastya should be brought in to collect and arrange the Tēvāra hymns lets in some light on the religious tendencies of that time. In the distant Java too, Agastya's name became intertwined with that of Śiva or Śiva Guru and assumed a sectarian importance of its own. The disillusion in the matter of the people worshipping the Śiva Guru images as the Agastya came, however, from an unexpected, but authoritative quarter. Dr. Vogel, the eminent Dutch Archaeologist, to whom the photographs of the Śiva Guru images were sent for inspection and identification, came to the correct conclusion that the images, all of which bore the Triśūla or the trident in their hands, were those of Śiva and not of Agastya. From my own inspection of the photos I was satisfied that all the images were Śiva's and that Dr. Vogel had given the correct verdict in the matter. Further, from the extract in page 55 of this paper from Bergaine's *Sanskrit Inscriptions of Champa,* it will be seen that Agastya journeyed to Cambodia to preach the worship of Śiva-liṅgam known as Śrī Bhadreśvara. The Śiva Guru images of Java are also known as Bhaṭṭāraka Guru images. Bhadreśvara of Cambodia and Bhaṭṭāraka of Java bear a close resemblance and may be variant forms of probably one name.* However, this is a matter for Sanskritists to decide.

Having been thus deified Agastya has come to evoke the greatest veneration among the people. This wave of piety led to a fresh recrudescence of myths and miracles which have now literally buried the original figure "ten thousand fathoms deep." One need not wonder at the fecundity of the imagination, from the most cultivated to the most ignorant, thus piling on the devoted head of Agastya layer after layer of legends of every description and colour. Almost every century had its quota to add and if the mass of tradition will in any manner supply a standard for determining the period of its growth and accumulation, at least a thousand years may fairly be allowed for the Agastya cult for its development to its present dimensions. Still in the field of psychology of a race, we cannot absolutely be sure of the validity of such surmises.[1] When a Geologist calculates

---

*These words are given the following meanings in Sir Monier William's Dictionary.

Bhadrēsvara = Various Statues or Liṅgas of Śiva.

Bhaṭṭāraka = Buddhist teachers and Śaiva monks.

1. Though the lore-dimension and quality of a tradition may give us an idea of its age, it is not at all possible to reach a correct standard for its age-determination. Judged either by quantity or quality of the materials that have gathered round certain popular heroes of recent dates handed down in ballad poetry of the day, such as Muttu Bhaṭṭan and Maturai Vīran of later myths, as Jai Singh and Khan Sahib

the age of a river by the successive layers of its alluvial deposit, he can positively be sure of his ground and conclusions for he is only dealing with unvarying physical forces that have at no point of time ceased working. Not so in the present case, where the thought and life of a nation are dealt with. There may be centuries of stagnation to be succeeded by others of unusual productivity and progress. The concatenation of circumstances which brings this about will defy the analysis of even the most accomplished historian. Yet with all these uncertainties which affect the later stages in the development of the Agastya cult, the tradition itself, according to the testimony of the early literature examined, cannot be taken behind the 5th Century A.D.

Intrinsic Improbabilities.

Viewing the Agastya tradition as a whole from its inception to its most recent development, it strikes us as an imaginative structure of magnificent proportions.

In the first place, the reason assigned for the Agastya exodus is too mythical for ordinary human belief. It is stated that he was sent to the South by God Śiva himself to equalize the balance of the southern half of the Globe with the northern. This primitive conception of the one portion of the earth tilting up and another sinking down—not certainly by any geological catastrophe—but by the sheer weight of the heavenly hosts gathered on the Himalayan top—is too puerile for serious criticism.

---

probably of the Carnatic Wars, as Katta Bommu and Ūmai Durai of the Poligar Wars of Tinnevelly, these recent legends seem to vie with the older, both in their elaborate character and in their mythic ingredients. So the massiveness of a tradition by itself is not a safe guide for the determination of its age.

Secondly, his residences in the South are too numerous and far distant one from another to be received as historical facts. He had his residence first on the southern outskirts of the Vindhya Mountains, next on the Mount Vaiḍūrya in the Satpura range, then on the Malakūṭa near Badāmi, then on the Pothiyil in the Pāṇḍya country, and lastly he appears to have migrated beyond the sea to the Malaya Hill in Sumatra and thence moved on to Siam and Cambodia.[1] Is it possible for one man to have displayed such catholicity of taste for a series of hill residences scattered throughout the Peninsular India and the numerous Indonesian Islands in the East ?[2]

Thirdly, a like improbability arises from Agastya officiating as the family priest of the Cālukya King

---

1. The following is found quoted by Mr. Gangoly in his article on Agastya published in the *Journal of the Mythic Society*, Vol. XVIII " That Brahmin Agastya, born in the land of the Aryans, devoted to the worship of Shiva, having come by his psychic powers in the land of the Cambodians for the purpose of worshipping the Shiva Lingam known as Shri Bhadreswara and having worshipped the God for a long time attained beatitude."—Bergaine's *Sanscrit Inscriptions of Champa*, 1893, LXV, p. 360.

2. Certainly a feeling of monotony will creep on the reader when he tries to run through the list of the Agastya residences in the various countries. The Mahāmalaya hill in the Malaya-Dvīpa and the Malayam Hill in Sumatra come to him merely as the second or third editions of Malakūṭa and Malaya of South India. In short, the principle followed appears to be that wherever a mountain or hill raised its head to the sky Agastya should be brought forthwith and located there. A hill without a Rishi of his eminence, in the view of the myth-makers, is almost a contradiction in terms.

Kīrtirāja of Lāṭa, N. Guzerat,[1] and of the Pāṇḍya King of the far away South.[2] Is it probable that in the conditions of South India in that early time when roads and other conveniences of travel did not exist that Agastya could have had such a large clientele of royalty to minister to?

Fourthly, judged by our ordinary standards, his exploits are mostly superhuman. Here human credulity is taxed a little too much. These performances hardly serve the purpose of establishing his historical character. Their cumulative effect after all seems to be the reverse.

Fifthly, his labours as the pioneer of Aryan civilization in the South and in the East have to surmount serious historical difficulties, before they are finally accepted. The aryanisation of the Mahārāṣṭra, then of the Karnāṭaka, then of the Tamil country, then of the Malay islands and lastly of Siam and Cambodia must each be assigned a few centuries at the least. No ordinary human being with a limited span of life of a hundred years or thereabouts could have coped with this gigantic task on a scale so colossal. Nor can it be pretended with due respect for the facts of history that the aryanisation of these various countries was simultaneous and could be compressed into the limited space of one identical century. These are a few of the difficulties presented to us by the Agastya tradition.

Thus we find that judged by the two fundamental tests referred to at the beginning *viz.*, (i) unbroken continuity of tradition with the past and (ii) absence of inherent

---

1. *Vide* the *Journal of the Mythic Society*, Vol. XVIII, p. 68.

2. *Vide* Sinnamanūr plate where Sundara Pāṇḍya is referred to as Agastya Śiṣya.

contradictions, the Agastya tradition breaks down completely.

Agastya—a Historic individual.

Yet attempts have not been wanting to rescue the sage from the atmosphere of pure myth and invest him with a sort of historic personality as that of Alexander the Great for instance. Mr. O. C. Gangoly in an article contributed to the *Journal of the Mythic Society*, calls him the leader of the Aryans in the great task of the aryanisation of Dakṣiṇāpatha. The Aryan immigration into Europe, into Iran, into North India, all appear to have been accomplished without a personal leader to direct the hosts. In the case of South India alone a leader was found necessary. Probably this last migration being the latest, the leader's name here has not fallen into oblivion. Whatever it be, the fiction of ascribing the origin and source of national movements and extensive social phenomena to single persons has unhappily not yet expired. In fact, national migrations are the results of social conditions and forces existing and working at the time and could in no way be ascribed to the thoughts and desires of individual men, however great they may be. In such movements communal or national leaders may arise and take a prominent part; when they do so, we should view them as acting under some sort of social necessity and compulsion and not as free agents drawing humanity after them as mere pawns or automata. Even the masterful Alexander the Great could not push his expedition further into the heart of India because of the opposition of his troops. He had to retrace his steps. The correct reading of the great characters of history is not to view them as isolated figures, standing on a pinnacle of their own and moulding the destinies of millions as it pleased them, but as the highest embodiments of the spirit of their times, the recognized channels through which the social forces had to work their way out for the accomplishment of their task set by the communal or national will. The ancient history of almost every country is filled with heroes. But to understand such heroes aright depends largely on the way in which their life-history is approached and studied. The appearance of the scientific method in history, superseding the ancient artistic one, introduces a new angle of vision and with it a new valuation of historical data. Where the pre-scientific recorder of facts laid too much stress on one human spirit embodied in a hero, as descending upon humanity from a sphere of its own, the scientific historian, grown perhaps a little impervious to the promptings of hero-worship, tries to dissect that spirit and read therein the reactions to its environment, to the peculiar stresses and pulls which had played about it and helped it on towards its development into a full-blown personality.[1] Science is not blind wonder but it is admiration built on positive analytic knowledge. It will untie the strands of a rope to its last filament to understand it aright before admiring it. In judging the national events of a time far

1. "As Theodore Merz has so well shown in the fourth volume of his monumental work of the Synthetic mode of regarding organisms, men and institutions, not as single things, self-contained and complete in themselves, but as merely nodes or meeting points of all the forces of the world acting and reacting in unlimited time and space."—William McDougall's '*Group Mind*' p. 2.

"People are always talking about originality ; but what do they mean ? As soon as we are born, the world begins to work upon us, and this goes on to the end. And, after all, what can we call our own except energy, strength and will ? If I could give an account of all that I owe to great predecessors and contemporaries, there would be but a small balance in my favour"—Goethe's Literary Essays (Spingarn's translation) pp. 256-257.

removed from ours, no doubt the mind, not being in possession of the social factors of those by-gone times, is disposed to catch hold of a hero, real or imaginary, here and there, and ascribe to him all the events of a particular epoch, which have to be somehow accounted for. This hankering after the creation of heroes may be artistically satisfying and even praiseworthy in its own way but must impede the growth of a true scientific history in our land.

Applying this principle of criticism to the Agastya tradition in South India and Further India, we find that the burden sought to be placed is too vast even for the Atlantean shoulders of an Agastya to bear. If he were a historical figure, as some are disposed to contend, his works should be judged by the ordinary canons of historic criticism. And what was his work in South India and outside? As already stated, it is nothing less than the introduction of Aryan knowledge and culture, Aryan beliefs and customs, Aryan religion and philosophy, in the Peninsular India from the Vindhyas to Cape Comorin, in the whole group of Indonesian Islands and in Siam and Cambodia still farther East. Even on the supposition that he was only the originator, the initiator of the movement, in all these countries and not the later architect of the works in different areas, one has still to admit that the aryanisation of all these countries was started simultaneously and should be compressed into the short space of a sage's life-time, say, a hundred or a hundred and fifty years at the most. Would any student of history stand by the implications of this astounding admission? Even the conversion of the Daṇḍakāraṇya into a habitable country for the Aryan colonists should have taken up two centuries on a moderate calculation. And another two centuries for the Karnāṭaka countries to be aryanised before Agastya could think of setting his foot in the Tamil land. Is it conceivable that

Agastya could ever have come to the Tamil land leaving behind him such a broad belt of territory as the Daṇḍakāraṇya and the Karnāṭaka peopled by alien tribes without first thinking of aryanising them and securing therein a firm base for his further progress? If colonisation were his motive, these forest regions offered him larger facilities than the populated area of the Tamil region. If on the other hand, he acted the part of a mere missionary to bring the light of his knowledge to the Tamilians, he might be supposed to have come direct to the Pāṇḍya country. But the tradition that seated him in the Malakūṭa range near Baḍāmi in the Kanarese country contradicts this supposition. Accordingly we have to assume that Agastya moved to the southern region stage by stage. In this scheme, however, his arrival at Pothiyil would be delayed by four or five centuries, at the least. Could Agastya have lived so long? To meet this difficulty, we have to assume either that Agastya was not an ordinary mortal or that there should have been many Agastyas to carry on the work of aryanisation. The former assumption removes the question from the pale of history and the latter contradicts tradition. All this difficulty is due to the champions of Agastya trying to mix up two opposing view-points, the mythical and the scientific. In judging of the historicity of Agastya, elementary canons of historic criticism demand that nothing of the impossibilities and improbabilities of mythic characters should be imported therein to vitiate our conclusion.

The upshot of the discussion regarding the historicity of Agastya then comes to this: that the aryanisation of the different countries of South India can in no way be ascribed to one common point of time but must be spread over a few centuries and that Agastya, if he were a historic character, could not have lived all that time to see his work even begun in those countries. He should have been long ago gathered to his forefathers before the later stages of the aryanisation work could be said to have been even started.

Whatever may be his historicity in the Ṛg Vēdic India of old, *i.e.*, in the Punjab or in North India, his translation to the Pothiyil of the South is a myth pure and simple and cannot be accepted as a fact in the primitive history of the Tamilians. Not only does it not square with the known facts of South Indian Literature and History but it contradicts them in many vital particulars.

Agastya—A Semi-Historic Personage.

It may still be contended that like Romulus of old, who founded Rome, Agastya might be considered as a sort of semi-historic personage. He might be taken as one of the primitive heroes of antiquity, whose features, though dimmed and distorted by tradition, have still a ring of reality about them. If he could not be brought before the foot-lights of history, he might at least be classed with those pre-historic figures who have worked at the foundations of a nation's culture. This, it may be conceded, is a perfectly legitimate hypothesis. On the stage of Aryan history or pre-history the sage fills a part, which no historian would be disposed to deny. If he had been left without disturbance in the Vedic *milieu* or in the period to which Rāmāyaṇa has a bearing, his character would not have suffered. But later myth-makers, with the strong instinct of hero-worship in them, would not allow him to rest there. He should be resurrected and brought again on another stage and that also at a far subsequent period to act another drama of momentous importance. The only difficulty here is one of chronology—the necessity of squaring the facts of one individual's life-time with those of the cultural periods of many nations in India and outside. The zealous labours of the mythologists have only gone to make a primitive historical character, only less and less historical down the ages, to the very verge of his losing that character altogether. Their blind zeal has done the greatest disservice to the ancient sage, whose very existence has thereby come to be doubted. In the limited view of considering literature as *the* standard for arriving at the civilization of a nation, indeed it is a far cry from the Ṛg Vēdic Literature which clusters about 1,500 B. C., to 2,000 B. C. to Tamil Literature which gathers round 100 A. D. How could a single character of the primitive history of these nations touch both these ends? This hiatus in chronology can be remedied only by supposing that there were more Agastyas at work than we are aware of. Apart from the Ṛg Vedic Agastya and the Agastya of the Rāmāyaṇa period, we require at least four more Agastyas to have begun the aryanisation of the Karnāṭic country, of Tamiḷakam, of the Indonesian Isles, and of Cambodia. Is it a rational hypothesis to make that one particular family should have specially given birth to a series of descendants on whom alone, of others, the duty of the aryanisation of the southern region devolved? Or were there many families of Agastyas or many individuals with a mere accidental coincidence in their names? Would it not be more rational to ascribe the continuity of the tradition to the unity of the name 'Agastya' which had struck root in the popular imagination by the labours of myth-makers and myth-preachers rather than to the unity of the family from which half-a dozen protagahists of culture should be derived?

Agastya—an Allegorical character.

We have now arrived at the last stage to which the progress of thought in this subject should inevitably take us. Scholars who feel that the Agastya problem in South Indian History bristles with many insurmountable difficulties have tried to modify the hypothesis not a little to reconcile it to certain stubborn facts. They realise that a historical Agastya in view of the stupendous volume of work that falls to his lot—not in one country but in many, not in one period but in many—is absolutely indefensible. Still to save the situation they try to read into the events of the aryanising epoch a dominant ideal, a persistent note, running through them all. Thus South Indian aryanisation becomes a beautiful long-drawn-out allegory in their hands and in such a poetic view of the whole process the critic is precluded from demanding the existence of a central historic personality. We have to take Agastya as neither more nor less than the embodiment of the ideal of the Aryan nation in their work of spreading their culture and knowledge to different countries of the South. This new school may urge that the Agastya legend need not be taken as treating of sober facts of history to be thrust into a strict chronological frame-work but must be viewed as the expression of a generalized type of activity which the Aryan colonists had been pursuing in the southern regions. Could not the spirit of Agastya—even after his bodily dissolution—be taken as animating his followers and driving them on to the accomplishment of the great task to which he had first set his hand ? Who will ever think of controverting this figurative way of interpreting South Indian History ?

Conclusion.

It is far from the purpose of this paper to disturb the complacency of those who believe that the sage Agastya lives to this day in the Pothiyil Mount and remains invisible to ordinary mortals; nor does it aim to convert another group which amuses itself by pouring the new wine of scientific history into the old bottles of mythologic tradition and imagines that the cause of both History and Tradition is somehow served thereby. Neither of these is in the least troubled by the oft-repeated taunt of the West that the Indians have no historical sense and discrimination. But fortunately for the reputation of India there is a numerous and growing band of Indian scholars, who do not flinch from applying the modern critical methods for the construction of a scientific history of their past. To this new and influential class, the positive facts and deductions, I have herein advanced about an ancient chapter in the history of the Tamilians, are commended for its consideration and judgment. The late Mr. Vincent Smith wrote : "Attention has been concentrated too long on the North, on Sanscrit books and on Indo-Aryan notions. It is time that due regard should be paid to the Non-Aryan element." I need scarcely add that the present is an attempt to carry out the wishes of that scholar in a subject wherein independent Non-Aryan testimony is imperative and should make itself heard.

APPENDIX I.

NOTE ON PTOLEMY'S 'BETTIGO.'

Dr. Caldwell correctly identified this with the Tamil Pothigai or Pothiyil. At the present day, Pothiyil is the name only of the southernmost promontory of the Western Ghats, later known also as Agastyarkūṭam. In Ptolemy's time, however, it appears to have had a larger signification. In Ptolemy's map, Mount Bettigo stands for the whole of the southern portion of the Western Ghats, *i.e.*, the Ghats running through the Tamil country of those days. It begins from the northern confines of Dimyrike, Tamiḻakam or the country of the Tamils, and runs down to a distance of nearly 300 miles. This range is also known as the 'Malayam' (lit. the mountain in Tamil). If in Ptolemy's days the term Pothiyil had signified only the southernmost peak, surely he would not have used it to denote the whole range of the mountains occupying some hundred miles. The restriction of the name Pothiyil or Malayam to the southern peak may probably have arisen at a far later day. Consequently, to import into the term 'Pothiyil' occurring in such works as *Puṟanānūṟu, Aganānūṟu*, etc., of the "Sangam" period, our modern restricted meaning is altogether wide of the mark and entirely misleading.* The

---

*As a glaring instance of this kind of unconscious misinterpretation, the following categorical summary of Poet Māmūlanār's reference by Dr. S. Krishnaswami Aiyangar in his *Beginnings of South Indian History* (pp. 90-91) may be quoted here. It runs thus:—"The fact of the invasion of the south by the Mauryas, the southernmost point reached being Podiyil Hill in the S. W. Corner of Madura." It is superfluous to point out that Dr. S. K. Aiyangar has thus sought to bring the Mauryas down to the present-day Pothiyil, being evidently misled therein by the restricted current denota-

A—9

earlier extended signification receives considerable support from the fact that the kingdom of Aioi (Aayi), the Pothiyil chieftain in Ptolemy's days, comprised not merely the country adjoining the present-day Pothiyil but extended far to the north and west as far as Melkynda (the Nelkynda of the *Periplus)*, the Nīrkunṛam or Niraṇam near Kōttayam in the northern district of Travancore. Mr. Cunningham in his *Geography of Ancient India* (p. 552) states that, in the Chino-Japanese map of India, the alternative name of Malayakūṭa, the southern portion of the Ghats, is given as Hai-an-men, which suggests a connection with Ptolemy's Aioi. Further, this extended earlier signification of the term 'Pothiyil' serves to give us the correct derivation of the name, besides shedding some light on the political divisions of Tamiḻakam in the early centuries. It is clear that it originally meant a common place, lying unappropriated by any one, though latterly it came to mean a place of public resort or meeting as மன்றம். It formed probably also the sheep or cattle range of a tribe of shepherds and cowherds known as *Pothuvar*. As this range of hills (Malayam) ran through the heart of the territories of the three Tamil Sovereigns of that period (Chēra, Chōḻa and Pāṇḍya) and separated their respective spheres of rule, it was considered by them a common belt of hill-region not belonging to any one king exclusively. As Aioi, the chieftain of a hill or forest region, was the earliest occupant

---

tion of that name. Further, the Mōkūr referred to in one of Māmūlanār's stanzas (Akam 251) as the capital of the chief whose recalcitrancy is said to have brought about the Mauryan invasion is not different, I should think, from Ptolemy's 'Magour' which is stated to be an inland city in the Paralia of the Sōretai (Chōḻas). Mōkūr thus falls outside the Pāṇḍya country. But here also Dr. S. K. Aiyangar seems to have been misled by Mahāmahopādhyāya Swaminatha Aiyar's erroneous identification of the place in his introduction to his *Puṛanāṇūru* as a town situate in the Pāṇḍyan territory. Whether the term Pothiyil occurring in this stanza refers to a hill at all is highly doubtful. But that need not be gone into at present.

of the lands on both sides of the Ghats (the village Āykkuḍi in the Shencōttah taluq on the eastern side of the Ghats will testify to Aioi's connection with the east), he seems to have appropriated the name and called himself the chieftain of Pothiyil and it is more than likely that his tribe was also known as the Pothuvar. This territory was afterwards merged in the Pāṇḍya kingdom and the Pāṇḍyas then came to be distinguished in literature as the 'lords of the Pothiyil'. At that time the Pāṇḍya country covered almost the whole of Travancore and Tinnevelly and Madura. But subsequent historical vicissitudes have brought about a shrinkage in their dominions and led to a corresponding restriction in the signification of the term 'Pothiyil' also. In later times, the western littoral of the ancient Chēra dominion became Malayalam-speaking and fell under the rule of numerous local chieftains, who wrested from the Pāṇḍyas by far the greater portion of the Pothiyil mountains and their adjoining regions. The Tamil name 'Pothiyil' consequently fell into disuse amongst them. The Pāṇḍyas, the sole surviving member of the ancient Tamil monarchs, then had to content themselves with the possession of the southernmost peak of the chain, which accordingly came to be known as the Pothigai. Thus Ptolemy's map and the Chino-Japanese maps have made it clear that the Pothiyil of the ancient Tamil poets about the early centuries of the Christian era is quite different from the Pothigai hill of the present day.

The following three lines from stanza 2 of *Puṟanānūṟu*,

> " அந்தி யந்தண ரருங்கட னிறுக்கு
> முத்தீ விளக்கிற் றுஞ்சும்
> பொற்கோட் டிமயமும் பொதியமும் போன்றே "

only go to confirm the interpretation I have herein sought to give to the term 'Pothiyil.' In these lines the

Poet institutes a comparison between the Himalayas and the Pothiyil mountain. The Himalayas, here, surely does not refer to a peak. It refers to the whole of a continuous chain of mountains. Naturally, a poet, who wants to bring in another mountain for comparison with this, is not likely to pitch upon a solitary peak or promontory in a chain of hills in Southern India, however sacred or otherwise important it may be. He must be taken to have had before his mind another range of mountains in the south which would stand comparison with the northern range. Thus early literary usage also makes it plain that Pothiyil refers to a chain of mountains and not to a particular peak in it, as it came to signify in later times.

I may also advert in this connection to the grammatical difficulty in interpreting 'Pothiyil' as a common belt of mountainous country unappropriated by the three Tamil kings of those days. Though the term பொதியில் like so many other terms in Tamil ending in 'இல்' signifies a place name, the phonetic rules of later grammarians state that பொது + இல் could become only பொதுவில் and not பொதியில். To escape this dilemma Dr. Caldwell split up the word into பொதி + இல் and interpreted the name as referring to a place of concealment. Apart from the fancied necessity of concealment—from whom or what Dr. Caldwell himself does not say—it is very unlikely that a metaphor should have been resorted to for naming a mountain where such terms as மறையில் or ஒளியில் would have answered the purpose even more suitably and with absolute directness. The difficulty which seems to have driven Dr. Caldwell to this fanciful derivation, however, could be got over by the supposition that the term itself arose at a very ancient period when the Tamil speech was in an amorphous condition as every spoken dialect should be expected to be and when the Tamil phonetic rules themselves had not acquired that regularity and rigidity which later on they came to assume in set grammatical treatises. Even these later grammarians had to show deference to such usage as is seen in பொதியில், கோயில், etc., and take it under the wing of what they are pleased to call இலக்கணப்போலி covering forms of words which in their opinion though not strictly grammatical are yet sanctioned by usage.

APPENDIX II.

TESTIMONY OF SCHOLARS *RE* DRAVIDIAN CIVILISATION.

After giving an account of the Aryan colonization of the Maratha country, Dr. Bhandarkar writes as follows :—

" But farther south and on the eastern coast, though they penetrated there and communicated their own civilization to the aboriginal races, inhabiting those parts, they were not able to incorporate them thoroughly into their own society and to root out their languages and their civilization. On the contrary, the Āryas had to learn the languages peculiar of those races and to adopt a portion at least of their civilization. Thus the Kanarese, the Telugu, and the Tamil and the other languages now spoken in Southern India are not derived from the Sanskrit but belong altogether to a different stock, and hence it is also that Southern Art is so different from the Northern. The reason why the result of the Āryan irruption was so different in Southern India from what it was in the North, appears to be that when the Āryans penetrated to the South there existed already well-organised communities and kingdoms."—*History of Deccan*, p. 10.

James Fergusson's *Study of Indian Architecture* contains the following reference about the Dravidian Architecture :—

" Here is a representation of a temple, at Badami, on the limits between the northern and southern architectural provinces. Any one at all familiar with the subject will at once recognise the difference between the two.

That on the left is a straight-lined low pyramid, divided into storeys, and adorned with pilasters, that on the right is curvilinear, with no trace of storeys or pilasters and instead of the domical form that crowns the one it terminates in a conventional fruit-like ornament. I know the people who erected the first must have been speaking Tamil or some of the allied languages when working upon it and that those who erected the other were speaking Bengalee or some tongue with a strong infusion of Sanskrit in its composition" (pp. 11-12).

From a study of the South Indian alphabets and languages Dr. Burnell comes to this conclusion :—

" The development of the early stages of the Grantha character is very difficult to trace, for the reason that the North Indian civilization, when it got far down in the Peninsula as the Tamil country, found there a people already in possession of the art of writing and apparently a cultivated language. Thus Sanskrit does not regulate the Tamil Phonetic system nor did it become more to the people than a foreign learned language."—*Elements of South Indian Palaeography.*

Prof. E. J. Rapson writes thus :—

"This extension is everywhere marked by the spread of Sanskrit and its dialects. It received a check in Southern India, where the older civilization and languages remain predominant even to the present day."—*Ancient India, p.* 9.

Apropos of the Dravidian race inhabiting South India, Dr. A. C. Haddon writes as follows:—

" Apart from language, there is a general culture which is characteristic of those peoples and after the elimination of the pre-Dravidians a racial type emerges with finer features than those of the aborigines and the conclusion seems evident that this was due to an immigrant people who reached India before 2000 B. C."—*The Races of Man.*

In his *Early History of India*, Dr. Vincent A. Smith writes as follows:—

"The ancient kingdoms of the far south, although rich and populous, inhabited by Dravidian nations not inferior in culture to their Āryan rivals in the north were ordinarily so secluded from the rest of the civilized world including Northern India, that their affairs remained hidden from the eyes of other nations; and native annalists being lacking, their history, previous to the year 800 of the Christian Era, has almost wholly perished" (p. 7).

Sir Walter Elliot adds the following testimony:—

"But although the Dravidians were not the earliest settlers, and although they have not been exempt and that in no small degree, from external influences, it is from them that the civilized part of the Dakkan derives its characteristic features in language and institutions. Among the latter may especially be noticed its monetary system and the coins in which it is expressed."—*Coins of Southern India* (p. 2).

APPENDIX III.

THE HYPOTHESIS OF MANY AGASTYAS.

While writing this paper, I had not sufficiently taken into account the tendency on the part of some scholars to make capital out of the bare possibility that more than one individual of the same name might have existed in the past as at present and played their role in the history of their land. But after going through a recent work, *The History of the Tamils* by Mr. P. T. Srinivasa Aiyangar, M.A., Reader in Indian History, I felt that I should have gone into the question at some length and offered detailed criticism on this favourite device often resorted to by certain Indian scholars for simply tiding over anachronisms, contradictions and irreconcilabilities turning up in the materials they happen to handle. It is, however, not possible to compress within the short space of an appendix the various considerations which should weigh with writers towards a cautious, not to say extremely limited, use of this hypothesis of plural personages going under one identical name in pre-historic times. Still, I shall try to indicate here a few of the major grounds which will show how risky it is to convert an exceptional method into one of general application.

Such writers as resort to it as a common step in their researches go on multiplying historical personalities, not for differentiating between separate individuals, admittedly historical, but with the sole object of parrying the arguments of the other side formulated against the historicity of such characters. These greet them from the most unlikely quarters, from times, places and circumstances not at all in keeping with their admitted antecedents. So far as these characters of ancient Indian history are concerned, chronology and geography, which form together the iron frame-work of history, have sometimes been twisted out of all recognition, if not wholly splintered and thrown together into an indistinguishable dust-heap. Two facts, to begin with, must give us food for serious reflection. Few will dispute that, in the first place, the phenomenon of plural personalities appearing under one identical name seems to occur frequently more in the history of India than in that of any other country in the world and, in the second place, more in the history of ancient India than of modern India. Why should this be so? The explanation, I think, lies not so much in the peculiar historical accidents of India as in certain psychological characteristics of its people, who react on the traditional materials of antiquity in a manner peculiar to themselves. It is very necessary to bear this in mind.

As a basis for my observations, I subjoin here a few extracts from H. H. Wilson's *Essays on Sanskrit Literature*, Vol. III and Mr. P. T. Srinivasa Aiyangar's *History of the Tamils.*

Essays on Sanskrit Literature, Vol. III.

P. 175. *Re* more than one Vararuchi :

"That the name of Vararuchi has in like manner been applied to different individuals might fairly be inferred from the practice thus described; but we have in this case a remarkable confirmation of our conjecture and find from the varying statements of several writers, that two, if not three persons of this denomination are celebrated in the literary history of the Hindus."

P. 189. *Re* more than one Sankarāchārya :

"The followers of Madhwacharya in Tuluva seem to have attempted to reconcile these contradictory accounts by supposing him to have been born three times; first at Sivuli in Tuluva about 1,500 years ago, again in Malabar some centuries later and finally at Padukachaytra in Tuluva no more than 600 years since; the latter assertion being intended evidently to do honour to their own founder, whose date that was, by enabling him to triumph over Sankara in a suppositious controversy."

History of the Tamils.

P. 30. *Re* more than one Rāvaṇa :

" Among others he (Kārtavīrya) defeated a Rāvaṇa, king of Lanka and imprisoned him in Mahiṣmati. This Rāvaṇa was certainly not the enemy of Rāmachandra who lived at least five hundred years later. Hence, the Rāvaṇa who was imprisoned by Kārtavīrya must have been an earlier Raja of that name or perhaps the guess of Dr. Sten Know is true that the name Rāvaṇa was but the result of the Sanskritization of Tamil ' Iraivan ' and merely meant a Tamil King."

Take along with this the foot-note:

" There was a' still earlier Rāvaṇa who fought with Anāraṇya, king of Ayōdhya."

P. 46. *Re* more than one Vālmīki :

" Probably this Vālmiki of the VII Century B.C. revised the Rāmāyaṇa of Vālmiki Pracētasa in classical Sanskrit and worked into it the concept of Rāma's being an incarnation of Viṣṇu."

P. 51. *Re* more than one Hanumān :

" Hanumān himself is said to have been the eighth great Sanskrit grammarian but this perhaps refers to a much later Hanumān."

P. 54. *Re* more than one Agastya :

" The first Agastya, husband of Lōpāmudra, a princess of Vidarba, was a contemporary of Alarka, king of Kāsi, who lived a little more than 20 generations before Rāma. Thus the earliest Agastya lived in the region immediate south of the Vindhyas."

* * * * * *

" But the Agastya whom Rāma met two yōjanas from Panchavaṭi could not have been the first Agastya, who lived about four centuries before Rāma's time, but must have been one of the later Agastyas ; for this Agastya of Rāma's day lived near the Gōdāvari, near which in his asrama, Rāma stayed on his way south."

* * * * * *

After referring to Agastya's residence on the top of the Malaya Hill (Coorg) the author writes:

" Hence this must have been inserted by a later poet who lived after the Agastyas had proceeded further south than the Agastya of Rāma's time and settled in the Tamil country."

* * * * * *

" In the Epic as in the Purāṇās, all the Agastyas are spoken of as one Agastya Rṣi, though different Agastyas resided in different places at different times."

These extracts are enough to convince the reader of the existence of peculiar difficulties besetting the path of a historian of ancient Indian Literature and traditions. If, from the shores of such literature and traditions, spectral forms of numerous Vālmīkis, Hanumāns, Rāvaṇas and Agastyas are thus found to accost the historian, surely he is apt to lose his bearings in the wide expanse of ancient Indian history unless he takes special care to keep a strict critical watch over this brood and banish such of them from his ken as are mere will-o-the-wisps.

Making the fullest allowance for the possibility and even probability of two or more historical personages going under one proper name, the question before the historian, especially ancient historian, is to see whether, even after a rigorous critical examination, there exist facts which would warrant his assuming for the explanation a different personality with an identical proper name, and not to rush at once to this handy expedient of multiplying personalities. We have seen how Agastya has come to figure in the ancient history of many countries in southern Asia and in many different centuries. Are we then to assume the existence of a separate Agastya for each country and also for each century in each country? This procedure does not seem to take into account the well-known fact that many characters have been created by poetic imagination or by mythic fancy or by religious megalomania. Are we to give to these spurious births a 'local habitation and a name' by admitting them into the gallery of historic personages? Turning to historical characters themselves, is it not a fact that later traditionalists have shifted some of these from their strict historical setting and made them play many different parts, in different places, and at different times? An impulse to blind hero-worship it is that furnishes the ground for so wrenching a character from its proper historical *milieu* and introducing it amidst new surroundings and conditions. Are we, here also, to resort to multiplying the original character as occasion requires? Then again, those who resort to this device exhibit an amazing credulity in the acceptance of even fictions as facts. No doubt, the common man is credulous by nature and acts on the principle that unless a statement is proved false it must be accepted as true. But that can hardly be the scientific frame of mind. Unless and until a proposition is proved true it has no credentials for acceptance. If the strength of history lies in its critically-tested and carefully-ascertained facts, is not the historian under the necessity of rigorously testing his facts before he tries to raise any theoretic structure on them or seeks to explain them. For instance, while the existence of Rāvaṇa himself as a historical character is not above doubt, what conceivable purpose can it serve to create two or three Rāvaṇas? While all the recensions of the existing Rāmāyaṇa text is in classical Sanskrit, why should a Rāmāyaṇa in Vedic Sanskrit be hypostasized and another Vālmīki created to become the author of that hypothetical Rāmāyaṇa? Along with this exhibition of 'primitive credulity' on the part of some investigators there is also a tendency to exhibit undue veneration towards ancient tradition and literature and to expect from them more than what the life and characteristics of the possessors of such tradition and literature would warrant us to expect. If in actual life we come across impostors and other unscrupulous characters, why could they not intrude now and then into the world of letters also? Are there not instances of deliberate forgeries committed in the name of well-known authors in the literary history of every country and at all times? Simply because a statement gets embodied in a literary work, does it become sacrosanct on that account? Should the critical method relax its rigour and go to sleep when that statement hails us from antiquity? On the other hand, the more an investigator recedes into the past the greater should be his care and circumspection in satisfying himself whether every fact rings true or not. If once that attitude is relaxed, history is likely to become more a fairy tale than a strictly scientific record of carefully-tested facts. Still, it may be urged that there are cases where the assumption of more than one historic character going under one identical name seems to be necessary. Such an assumption, however, can be resorted to only in cases where strict historical conditions vouch for it. The creation of a dozen Agastyas to answer all the differences brought about by historic conditions and then to formulate the existence of a family of Agastyas to which all of them are to be traced is scarcely a justifiable procedure. In fact, this delectable method of creating a number of Agastyas, Rāvaṇas and Hanumāns and of an equal number of families to go under such generic proper names is too vague and indefinite for practical application. What does this family name connote in India ? Does it cover only a simple family (gens), or a group (phratry) composed of many families, or a whole tribe composed of such groups? If gōtra names, such as Atri, Bhāradvāja, be considered as family names, millions of the present-day Āryans could be distributed under a few gōtras and be considered as the Atris and Bhāradvājas of this century. But this would hardly serve the purpose of any clear identification of the individuals concerned. Thus the gōtra name will in no way serve our purpose and need not be resorted to as signifying a definite individual in any period of our history except the first founder of a particular gōtra. Is it not a little disconcerting that proper names intended to identify definite individuals should thus be converted into indefinite generic names for uncontrolled and even whimsical application ?

In this connection, the attention of these scholars may be drawn to a very wholesome principle of scientific procedure called "the Occam's Razor." Where one hypothesis is sufficient to explain adequately a number of observed facts, it is a vicious scientific procedure to formulate more than one hypothesis for the same purpose. Applying this principle to the phenomenon of many Agastyas appearing in the history of different countries and at different times, are we to go on assuming the existence of separate Agastyas for each country and for each century ? Or are we to ascribe the whole phenomenon to a common psychological characteristic of the races concerned—the strong tendency to hero-worship ingrained in them ? It is very likely that the first Agastya was a historic character but the subsequent Agastyas were all the result of popular imagination catching hold of an ancient hero and spinning round him all sorts of stories. Where such a solitary hypothesis as this is sufficient to account for all the facts of the case, is it not a violation of legitimate scientific procedure to go on creating Agastyas *ad libitum* to suit the multiplicity of historical circumstances turning up ? If anywhere, here it is that the necessary pruning, insisted upon by the old Logician, should be effected.

The following observations of Mr. Bhagabat Kumar Goswami made in the introduction (pp. xxxii-xxxiii) of his work, the *Bhakti Cult in Ancient India*, will, I think, be of interest as bearing upon the pruning he attempts to do in the case of Vyāsa :—

"Whenever a new system of thought arose in Hindustan, it was not only sought to be based upon some teaching of the Vedas but the name of Vyāsa was generally sought to be connected with the department of thought some way or other while the names of the Vedic seers themselves were utilised for similar purposes wherever necessary and possible. This was specially the case after the Buddhistic onslaught on Vedicism. Vyāsa then figured as a writer of philosophical commentary *Yogabhasya*, an author of a philosophical system, Brahma Sūtra, an author of a Smṛti system, Vyāsa Smṛti, a writer on polity, a writer on Astrology. He was again claimed as the author of all the Purāṇas and to crown all, the author of the whole of the greatest

Epic *Mahābhārata*. When not the original author, he was often traditionally claimed as connected some way or other with the authors of the other systems, who themselves in most cases bore the sacred names of or claimed some affinities with the old Vedic seers. To seek therefore to fix a historic age from some alleged connection of the name of Vyāsa or a Vedic seer is to court disaster. We must leave Veda Vyāsa at about 3,100 B.C. and allow other Vyāsas to take care of themselves."

To the Vasiṣṭhas, who figure as numerously as the Vyāsas, Mr. F. E. Pargiter feels justified in giving a different treatment. Being committed to the position of finding greater authenticity in the Kṣatria tradition than in the Brahman, he is forced to conclude that the later Vasiṣṭhas were as historical as the kings with whom they lived. He is not disposed to apply the pruning knife to the requisite extent and grapples with the Purāṇic traditions to extract from them some genealogical facts for the construction of history. How in this heroic attempt he gets hopelessly entangled in the legendary quagmire will be seen if one tries to follow the identifications and discriminations of the many Vasiṣṭhas he makes in pp. 203-211 of his work *Ancient Indian Historical Tradition.* He dismisses the first two Vasiṣṭhas (the mind-born son of Brahma and one, the contemporary of Ikshuwaku) as mythical, and considers the later Vasiṣṭhas as historical. But when we find these later Vasiṣṭhas described as having most of the characteristics attendant on their mythical prototype, we have to doubt the validity of the procedure, adopted by Mr. F. E. Pargiter in the valuation of the testimony of the Purāṇic annalists—accepting it as trustworthy in one portion and rejecting it as entirely worthless in another. How, for instance, could each one of the fourth, the fifth and the seventh Vasiṣṭhas possess Arundhati as his wife, the Arundhati, the companion of their mythical progenitor ? Much the safer rule in such cases would have been to accept all or none. Nothing in these regions will enable us to distinguish between Tweedledum and Tweedledee. It is true that by arranging the goodly company of Vasiṣṭhas as Vasiṣṭha I, Vasiṣṭha II, etc., in an arithmetical series, some sort of order is introduced into chaos; but how can one be sure that it is an order of a real series and not an imaginary one ? To say that these have been referred to by their gōtra names merely is to clutch at a straw, or even worse, a shadow. The works in which these traditions are embodied must be taken either as contemporary records or later compilations. If contemporary, the authors should naturally be expected to distinguish the character they write about by giving the personal name and other biographical details which could distinguish their character from others of the same gōtra. At any period of time the Purāṇas treat of, there should have been living a very large number of Vasiṣṭhas claiming their descent from one of the seven progenitors of the race. Would any contemporary writer leave the character he seeks to glorify in the haze and uncertainty of a generic name ? If, on the other hand, the works are considered as later compositions, as presumably they are in spite of their prophetic manner, the authenticity of their statements so far as personal identifications are concerned gets more and more attenuated and loses in value as we recede from the times treated of. Hence, a Vasiṣṭha going under a gōtra name, unless he is rendered distinct by authentic details of a personal or historical character, is little better than a figment of the writer's imagination conjured out of the name of a legendary hero or the idol of a literary coterie.

Granting, however, the legitimacy of the method—the assumption of a gōtra name to explain away a number of characters under one denomination coming to us from the distant past—the question will naturally arise how this method will help us in solving such a problem as the four or five Auvais appearing in different periods of Tamil

Literature. To what gōtra did the original Auvai, the Tamil Poetess, belong? Or should we resort to some other method to save the historicity of all the Auvais figuring in Tamil literary history? The truth of the matter is that Mr. Pargiter's tenderness towards traditions as a whole has, I fear, made him a little too prone to ascribe objective reality even to subjective creations. He seems to have wholly expunged the subjective factor as an agent in the creation of personalities and perhaps may have thought that novelists are all of modern growth, the old world having none to show. However, the more we push our way into antiquity, the more are we brought into contact with an imagination of an unbridled type. Reason seems to have been a slow growth of millenniums of tardily accumulated experience and painful labour. As against this, it was all easy for imagination to go to work. Hence it is that imagination got a start over slow-developing Reason, the results of which are visible even to this day. Few will doubt the abstract probability of traditions containing truths, but, when a large masses of them are thrown into the melting-pot of a poet's imagination or overwrought religious feeling or sectarian prejudice, to expect reality or truth to emerge therefrom unscathed is to expect the impossible.

APPENDIX IV.

WORKS CONSULTED.

ENGLISH.

1. Prof. MaxMuller's *History of Ancient Sanscrit Literature.*
2. Dr. Washburn Hopkins'. *The Great Epic of India.*
3. Dr. Bhandarkar's *Early History of Deccan.*
4. The *Periplus of the Erythræan Sea* (McCrindle's translation).
5. Prof. A. A. Macdonell's *History of Sanskrit Literature.*
6. Prof. Ihering's *The Evolution of the Aryans.*
7. Ptolemy's *Geography of India and Southern Asia* (McCrindle's translation).
8. Travancore State Manual.
9. Mr. F. E. Pargiter's *Ancient Indian Historical Tradition.*
10. Dr. Caldwell's *Comparative Grammar of the Dravidian Languages.*
11. Prof. Seshagiri Sastri's *Essay on Tamil Literature.*
12. Dr. Burnell's *Elements of South Indian Palæography.*
13. Prof. E. J. Rapson's *Ancient India.*
14. Mr. L. W. King's *Babylonian Religion and Mythology.*
15. Dr. Vincent A. Smith's *Early History of India.*
16. Prof. William McDougall's *Group Mind.*
17. Gœthe's 'Literary Essays' (Spingarn's translation).
18. Dr. A. C. Haddon's *The Races of Man.*
19. The *Epigraphia Carnatica,* Vol. II.
20. The *Journal of the Mythic Society,* Vol. XVIII.
21. The Catalogue of the Oriental Manuscripts Library, Egmore, Madras.

22. Dr. S. K. Aiyangar's *Beginnings of South Indian History.*

TAMIL.

1. *Paripāṭal.*
2. *Pattuppāṭṭu.*
3. *Puṛanānūṛu.*
4. *Naṛṛiṇai.*
5. *Tolkāppiyam.*
6. *Ilakkaṇakkottu.*
7. *Vīrasōḻiyam.*
8. *Tiruvāymoḻi.*
9. *Tēvāram.*
10. *Aganānūṛu.*
11. *Jīvakachintāmaṇi.*
12. *Chilappaṭikāram.*
13. *Pannirupaṭalam.*
14. *Puṛapporuḷveṇbāmālai.*
15. *Agapporuḷ Viḷakkam.*
16. *Divākaram.*
17. *Tiruviḷayāṭal Purāṇam.*
18. *Kānchi Purāṇam.*
19. *Sīkāḷattipurāṇam.*
20. *Tāṇḍavarāyaswāmi's Works.*
21. *Pērakattiyattiraṭṭu (Rao Saheb Bhavanandam Pillai's Edition).*
22. *Kantappurāṇam.*
23. *Kācikāṇṭam.*
24. *Tirukuṛṛālattalappurāṇam.*
25. *Tiruvēnkaṭattalappurāṇam.*
26. *Tirunelvēlittalappurāṇam.*
27. *Kuḍantaippurāṇam.*
28. *Mayilaippurāṇam.*
29. *Vētāranyapurāṇam.*
30. *The Chentamil, Vol. XIX.*

INDEX.

W

Y